THE AGE OF REASON

OF

REASON

(1931-2015)

THE AGE
OF
REASON

(1931-2015)

A Journey beyond the Theories
of Albert Einstein, Stephen Hawking,
and Thomas Paine

William Moreira

THE AGE OF REASON (1931-2015)
A JOURNEY BEYOND THE THEORIES OF ALBERT EINSTEIN,
STEPHEN HAWKING, AND THOMAS PAINE

iUniverse books may be ordered through booksellers or by contacting:

iUniverse
1663 Liberty Drive
Bloomington, IN 47403
www.iuniverse.com
1-800-Authors (1-800-288-4677)

ISBN: 978-1-4917-8119-7 (sc)
ISBN: 978-1-4917-8121-0 (hc)
ISBN: 978-1-4917-8120-3 (e)

Library of Congress Control Number: 2015919682

Print information available on the last page.

iUniverse rev. date: 12/1/2015

In Memory

Carol Jacqueline Moreira (1962–1996)

Nothing reaches as deeply into our minds as moral pain, as the tragic death of our child, especially after thirty-three marvelous years.

I cried for two weeks and couldn't pilot my Cessna for six months, and then one morning, as I was staring at the clouds from her bedroom window with a hollow heart because she wasn't there but maybe up there, I heard her voice loud and clear:

"Pappy, life is beautiful. It doesn't matter what, because we are God's children."

Was it a daydream or maybe just my mind in search of hope as a consolation? Was it God's mercifulness?

If wasn't for the concept of a Creator as perfect as the universe, because there is no other way of imagining it, life wouldn't be worth one minute of breathing.

That night, I reached as high as my wings could take me, and there I said my prayers, this time to Him and to her. I knew both were in the celestial dimensions where we will all be, because when love is involved, there can never be an eternal separation.

William Moreira (Canno)—a faithful father

CONTENTS

PREFACE

I had to go above and beyond the altar of ignorance, blind faith, religion, atheism, nihilism, science, popes, terrorism, Stephen Hawking's negativity, Albert Einstein's childishness, and Thomas Paine's common sense.

I heard God say, "Son, you finally reached Me not to beg or cry but as your Creator." "In My Father's house are many mansions." Christ gazed at heaven's door as I followed Him.

This book is my gift to you all as I reach my eighty-fourth year of material and spiritual experiences. It wasn't and isn't easy, but it gave me the knowledge that we are born, suffer, and die to spiritually evolve and achieve eternal life.

A Life in Pictures

Washington (DC) Author doing
a interview for the Brazilian
Consulate (35-years old) **1968**

New York City (NY) with
wife Gladys and CAROL as a
baby (22 years-old) **1955**

Palm Springs (CA-) his plane CESSNA 182 RG (65 years-old) **1998**

PRESS CARD, Brazil) (23 years-old) **1956**

JOURNALIST ID (Brazil) 20 years-old - **1953**

1 For a Better Life on Earth

Forgive your enemies as I have forgiven mine. My former enemies have become unhappy being my enemies. That's made me happy.

Forgive people in your life, even those who aren't sorry for their actions. Holding on to anger only hurts you, not them. Be a reflection of what you like to see in others; if you want honesty, give honesty. If you like respect, give respect. If you want love, give love.

Words are free. It's how you use them that may cost you. Always think before you speak or write.

2 Theories and Intelligence Mean Nothing If They Don't Help Us

I went to buy some lobster in Aventura, Florida, for dinner. I was supposed to be the chef that night, but when I saw an issue of *Popular Science*, my guests had to settle for my grandson's cooking. I was eager to read "100 Mysteries of Science Explained: Experts Uncover the Secrets of the Universe from end-of-the-world scenarios to disappearing bees and beyond, and as a bonus, Featuring Dark Matter—Black Holes—Time Travel."

Can I now just use my pen to save the world from the fantasies of dreamers who don't dedicate time and brainpower to help our ailing planet? That's my question for those who are blind in faith and maybe with below-average IQs.

They were and are being glorified as geniuses but don't help solve Earth's problems today much less problems that could be handled only by spirits such as Einstein. The grotesque picture of him sticking out his tongue reflects the theories he spent his life dedicated to creating to come up with his own theories fan club.

Geniuses are those who labor to finding solutions for our ailing planet's problems and diseases that are eating humans and animals from the inside out while antibiotics are losing the battle. Other "geniuses" spend money and intelligence building war machines to eliminate our race and are applauded by the masses. They ignore the fact that Florida's Everglades and its freshwater are being infiltrated by salt water.

Why should I worry about what's going on? I have only a few more years left in my earthly body. Others tell us not to worry about spending our last pennies on ourselves, but our children and grandchildren are waiting to find out what's in our wills though they don't call us for months.

I read a *National Geographic* story, "Destination Pluto!" "Almost a decade in flight, the New Horizons spacecraft is approaching the enigmatic dwarf planet. What it will find there is anybody's guess." But Earth and the extermination of humanity should be everyone's worry. I would have applauded Nadie Drake and her dear father, who have spent much energy to save our descendants with articles not from Pluto: "Small, cold, and absurdly far away, Pluto has always been selfish with its secrets."

My reply is, "God, please save the Earth." Our planet is dimming. Pollution is being talked about as was the Korean War armistice, but that took so long that soldiers and civilians suffered from 1950 to 1953, and Earth's problems and the armistice haven't been solved.

The first time I flew from Rio to New York was about sixty-three years ago. I was in my twenties and was taking a Lockheed four-engine L-1049 Super Constellation there. See the picture I took from inside as we were almost touching Sugar Loaf Mountain, 1,500 feet tall. It was carrying sixty passengers; I flew for twenty-six hours at 375 mph at an altitude of 20,000 feet. It stopped three times to refuel. Now, a plane can make the trip in eight hours at an altitude of 40,000 to up 50,000 feet, almost turbulence-free, and carry 500 souls.

That all sounds great—carrying more people in less time using a fraction of the fuel, but the geniuses should stop working on their ideas of reaching places billions of light-years away and focus on our critical, daily-bread problems, all the calamities and nightmares the people on this planet face today as maybe will be no tomorrow.

Modern cars such as Cadillacs, Mercedes Benzes, Chryslers, BMWs, and so on, get only fourteen to less than thirty miles per gallon, and billions of gallons of gas pollute the ground while billions more gallons of fuel pollute the atmosphere by aviation and industry, create acid rain, and spoil our drinking water. Why didn't Einstein put some of his IQ to work on developing atomic engines for the ships that crisscross the planet so they wouldn't pollute the seas? We'll soon see global wars for water.

We have free will, but we don't all have great intelligence. If we did, there would be no wars, pollution, and so on. That's why religions are great; they offer paradise in the future to us, who are in the present.

Fantasies and dreams were great when I was very young. World War

II was something only adults talked about then. I just wanted to play, read cartoons, paint, and have fun. It was later in my life that I matured and wanted the knowledge I'd need to face humanity's challenges.

I wanted those super geniuses to quit thinking about preparing Mars as our new home as if it were just across the pond, because that would do nothing for animal life here, and Mars is way too cold and lacks oxygen. I could imagine the NASA announcement: "Enterprise Mars, built as Earth's last hope, is boarding now. Will the last five thousand earthlings line up? We've made Earth a hell with no drinking water and polluted air, and we have no more petroleum, as was predicted by the prophets. Please have your boarding tickets ready."

I put my thoughts on paper as fast I can before they evaporate. This is the same way Earth is being destroyed. Supposedly, we live in a huge city nestled between mountains and have no contact with other civilizations, but we have fertile land and clean water. We feel blessed by God.

Then along comes a genius who tells us we have to go up miles to search for our creator and find out his secrets. Ignorance takes over, and most of us try to do just that in the name of cosmology. Meanwhile, as the population increases, so does anarchy and pollution and water that's no good for drinking. Because of deforestation, our supply of oxygen is low. Because of the lack of spirituality and an abundance of greed, the valley's population is doomed just as the Mayans were millennia ago. Today, thanks to high technology and low intelligence, not one civilization but the whole planet is doomed. The only places we can go are heaven or hell—take your pick.

This inspiration came at a quarter to seven one morning after I spent twenty-six hours on my laptop trying to leave some insight behind for those who are looking for it.

As a reward to myself for celebrating my eighty-fourth birthday and this book (August, 25, 2015) I went on a cruise aboard the *Costa Favolosa* to the northwest area of Russia. We had flown on Air Berlin from Miami to Denmark (there we enter the ship for 7 days) to Sweden, Estonia, Saint Petersburg (Russia), Latvia, Germany and back to Denmark on a total of fourteen days.

Years ago I spent thirteen days in Saint Petersburg, Moscow, and Kiev. I had been on a special tour while communism was already losing its power because of its being an anti-God system. But now I was in the company of four of my adult grandchildren, who are full of energy but my 80 years old wife keep the eyes on me. I did not run after them; I stayed cool in the shadows because of my age.

I feel that my time is getting shorter and that I cannot stretch out my time on our beautiful material world. I feel more than love for those I will leave behind; I hope for better days for them and everyone else not taking immediate leave of our planet.

When I hear geniuses spouting off about their latest theories such as Stephen Hawking and his time-travel ideas, as the same to the late Einstein, it makes me feel I'm in kindergarten again and forced to listen to the big-mouthed kids trying to call attention to themselves while mocking others.

Our existence is our only existence because the past is the present rolled up to yesterday; how could we jump into the future, which is always a fantasy? Billions of years are right behind us, and we can travel to the beach, but we have to do it in real time. If an outer-space journey at the speed of light takes fifty years round trip, your friend of twenty-five years will be seventy-five years older upon your return. Distance and speed have nothing to do with our aging process as much as the air we breathe, because time has no effect on speed, which is a real-time event. Even as our bodies go, our spirits will stay around in a dimension or two or three, but that will be in present time or end up irrelevant.

Some years ago, the TV program *One Step Beyond* showed people going to the future or the past, and *Twilight Zone* ran at the same time, the late fifties and the early sixties. The series *Star Trek: Enterprise* in 1966 was a marvelous series, but it was Carl Sagan's *Cosmos* that showed us our fantastic existence here and to infinity. He departed to the cosmos at an early age (1934–96) leaving us asking our Creator why the good ones leave us prematurely while the bigmouths stay.

University diplomas and political power alone won't solve humanity's problems; incompetents in the wrong jobs will accomplish nothing, and incompetent efforts will not put the bread—the solutions—we need on the table.

If Einstein wasn't drinking when he came up with his theories, he must have been overdosed on caffeine or wildly dreaming. We're all on the same planet and were born the same way, but our IQs are different as our bodies. A spirit Einstein might have surpassed light speed going into dark matter; spirits aren't restricted that way. He could have learned about dark matter in a dream and then woke up thinking he could conquer the future. But to dream is only to hope for the future; we must face reality because our existence is on the line.

Speed as relative to time doesn't take us to the future as the future doesn't exist. Speed gets us elsewhere measured in miles but only in present time. Time on Earth is the same as time anywhere in the universe. Going at the speed of light, a particle takes us just as a river's current take us downstream, not into the future but a distance related to the speed at which we travel regardless of what Hollywood tells us.

Are there beings billions of light years in the future? No. Otherwise, they would exist or we would be just illusions. Let's stop these childish games and think like intelligent adults; let us not stick out our tongues and leave our hair uncombed and think that's funny. Let's focus on staying involved in the world and with others and avoid coming up with make-believe, abnormal theories.

Sometimes in the still of the night, as I flew off in my small Cessna, I saw only emptiness above. I was not flying into the future but to somewhere else. I witnessed our vast universe but never thought that my speed would let me penetrate into what was to be. That was reality, not a dream.

The *Concorde* prototype was manufactured by the Russians and broke the sound barrier as it was taking passengers from Moscow to Rio de Janeiro. But according to a famous Brazilian tabloid newspaper, it had accelerated to a billion times the speed of light and had landed somewhere else in the galaxy. When, according to that tabloid, the pilot concluded he was lost because his angle of attack had led him out of Earth's gravitational pull. He had entered the cosmostream rather than the jet stream (our jet stream is wind, not light). His speed indicator had gone so high that it had burst into pieces. His only option was to reverse course and reenter the cosmostream. He landed in Rio and saw the statue of Christ blessing the lost ones.

His was the first dreadful flight of this expensive white elephant. The *Concorde* had become a spacecraft for an hour. He was questioned by NASA, the United States, France, Germany, England, Brazil, and naturally Russia, because its reputation was at stake. The plane had been off the radar for an hour and was one hour late to Rio. The poor souls kept their mouths shut, and the passengers hadn't worried about it; they had been busy drinking champagne.

According to the tabloid, the only passenger onboard who had noticed the pilot's mistake and the aging of the passengers was Albert Einstein, who luckily had a hand-held GPS he used to check the speed of the jet; it had reached 186,000 miles per second. The biggest brain in the world knew that light consisted of particles, but he didn't talk because his tongue had frozen up with emotion.

He was taken to Albert Einstein Hospital in São Paulo for evaluation, and he wrote with chalk on a blackboard to explain his experience of going into the future. Everyone believed him because of his phenomenal theories about atoms; he was acclaimed even though he had become childish at his advanced age.

Still according to the newspaper, after leaving the hospital, Einstein vanished. Everyone realized it had been a ghost; he had died in 1955. Because it was 1977, this demonstrated he couldn't beat aging going into the future or into the past; he had to stay in the present. I saw ghosts as a young boy. In all our sixty-plus years of marriage, my wife kept a lit candle to guarantee my spiritual peace or to guarantee my reasonableness.

Logic, common sense, and reason can help us do good for society, but we don't all share in those attributes. Some people carry around immature minds and say things enough times that they end up believing them and convincing others of them. Famous people in history have attracted legions of fanatics following them for this reason and have perpetrated tragedy after tragedy.

Our life on Earth is a comedy, as said Dante; we laugh and cry, but we must stop glorifying nonsense. We must look at the future through rational eyes and not worry whether light is a wave or particles or both, as said Einstein. Sooner or later, someone will come up with another theory, and why not? Just like "One or two sugars?" we can choose.

This book's cost might be as much as a cheap glass of wine in a fancy joint, and reading this book may have caused you to bump into a lamppost, but this book as *The Age of Reason* will bring more sense to your life. Besides, I'm not interested in the money. My reward will be in my doing battle with all the negativity in life.

3 Tears from the Author

I f you don't have values or beliefs, you won't be able to accomplish your mission or dream for a better day and an afterlife. Our bodies are marvelous bridges between the carnal and the eternal world. If you don't grasp this, you'll age faster and feel all the negatives such as Hawking's idea that nature has no intelligence and free will. Be prepared to have your guts blasted out by a hurricane.

If you are in doubt, an atheist, someone who has never seen a spirit that has shaken the moral fiber out of you, finish this book and we'll talk. I don't have your email, but you have mine. If we hold on to blind faith, we will be blind even with our eyes open; our sight won't go farther than our noses to the horizon.

I tossed the first eighty or so pages of this book into the ocean from onboard the cruise ship *Lyrica*. It was December 11, 2014, and I was on my way from Rio to Buenos Aires. I pitched the pages an hour after I had finished three days of writing what was to be my last book. I screamed at God because I had been writing a book for everyone, but I had come to the conclusion that it was easier for Stephen Hawking to go to heaven, Albert Einstein to admit he was wrong, or the Vatican to stop clerical abuse of children than it was for me to finish writing it. Average people are more interested in keeping their noses in cell phones, going to church to beg for or demand something from our Creator, and not loving each other in the name of charity as millions starve.

Religion would call this a revelation: I was in my teens and was an avid reader. I opened an old, stained book whose cover was missing. Out of curiosity, I read some articles and discovered it was a book on deep, spiritual philosophy. I still don't know what book it was, but I have it in my soul; it was a message from beyond our horizons.

Lately, as a senior journalist and writer, I began writing books and letters to politics and religion leaders about the immorality and disrespect that affects us all. It was sixty-eight years after I had read that book, but in a moment of stress, it came back to me. My memory of it convinced me we are more than flesh and bones.

As I sent my comments on *The Age of Reason* to editors, the tragedy in Paris at the offices of the satirical *Charlie Hebdo* occurred on January 11, 2015. Twelve people were killed there, and four more elsewhere. The crime put France and other countries on alert against terrorism. Had this been an attempt on freedom of speech?

Perhaps it could have been avoided, but the law of cause and effect is universal. We shouldn't analyze the tragedy in Paris without blind faith but with reason; unreasonable people see only one side of the coin.

We could ask, "Is it wrong to expose religious and social ills?" but I will put this question in another form: "Will God or humanity find fault with authors or satirists who expose others' wrongdoing in society, religion, politics, personalities, and so on as for their amusement and to inflict moral pain on others?" It depends on your motive. If you want only to create scandal or satisfy a personal grudge by showing the worst of religion (even cults) or society, then it is wrong, and those involved will pay the price, sometimes with their lives. A writer, satirist, or comedian who takes pleasure in pointing out others' wrongs for its own sake will be held responsible for that; it's only a matter of time.

Is it wrong to study others' flaws? Yes, if you do it simply to criticize them or reveal their flaws; that shows a lack of compassion. If you study others' flaws to learn about and correct your own faults, that could be useful. But you have to consider if you could be accused of the same faults. The only reason for this kind of study is to acquire virtue. Is someone miserly? Be charitable. Is someone proud? Be humble. Is someone harsh? Be gentle. As Jesus said, see the log in your eye before you point out the motes in others' eyes. Many in my profession as well as satirists and humorists without high ethical principles eventually harvest what they sow because of the law of cause and effect. *Charlie Hebdo* is a serious, sad example.

The distressed souls seeking answers to life's problems do so in a marvelous world full of beauty and tragedy; we all face the deaths of our bodies, which many think is our only existence. Few can see or communicate with spirits; those who do are generally only one of two parties involved in this, as was the case with John in Revelation. My mother and I were blessed with this phenomenon or miracle.

I have been called a blunt, sharp-minded, straightforward genius who was blessed and an unreasonable, dumb, atheistic, godless, badly informed, Brazilian-nuts religion writer and journalist with no logic at all. Those adjectives came from those who based their thinking on blind faith and the one book imposed on them by religious leaders; they were lost at their own crossroads.

I was defended by some intellectuals who relied on reason. Their attitudes kept me writing, and that kept me from getting bored and feeling negative. Maybe you heard that singing keeps our sorrows away; that's true because when we hear music, our worries open our hearts to merry thoughts. Classical music will help you digest your meals and close your ears to the bigmouths.

Many friends have told me I was trying to save the world, but not even Jesus could do that. They attempt to persuade me to just travel like a regular soul, enjoy life, and keep my pen in the drawer, but they don't realize I can do all these things. I just keep both eyes open as if I were flying a plane. If we were never challenged, we'd quickly end up bored. We'd be like a marriage without children to bust our chops, as the Brits say.

No one has ever walked my thorny roads, but I never lost my charming, charismatic attitude. We must never use our problems to bring hell to others; that shows a lack of love. It won't help anyone; it will just make things more difficult for all involved. I always hold bad news to myself, avoid gossip, and run from hearsay. Just like the Lamentation Wall in Jerusalem, I listen to the tumult and crying but don't respond. When someone sends me a negative email, I hit delete. If the message comes over the phone, I disconnect the phone for a few days. What do you do when you walk into a room with a foul odor? You leave.

Instead of wishing to hell someone you don't like or doesn't belong to your religion, use your brains to figure out if you're standing on hot lava that could shatter your dreams or even your life. I'm talking about your family as well as your enemies. Ahead is the darkness, a void that keeps you up all night holding tight to your holy book but without answers; you're as hopeless as the whole planet and the galaxies that could be devoured by Stephen Hawking's black holes or Satan's meteor. Your hope of reaching heaven could be shattered. Becoming spiritualized by logic and common sense is our only defense in God's universe.

A book means nothing if you don't read it and take in its wisdom; it could help you to love life as it is and suffer less or even happily. When I was young, I chose books that fulfilled my thirst for wisdom from every direction; that's what allows me to advise those with no degrees and those with many, those with no medals or those with plenty, those with noses to the grindstone or noses pointed up to the heavens.

Concentrate on this book's content, not just its words. Keep it in your thoughts and learn to reason your way out of the labyrinth; blind faith won't help you do that. Our time on Earth is limited, and nothing can be done tomorrow if we're not here to do it.

Don't give up hope, which is all we have. For eighty-four years, I gazed at Christ as He gazed on the infinity above Him. I did so at fifteen thousand feet on my Cessna Skylane above Manhattan on clear winter nights, and it paid off. Jesus didn't give up seeking the way out of our suffering, and He found it among the galaxies. I'm getting closer to Him.

There's no law against lowercasing *he* as a pronoun for God, but when writers anywhere do so, they cringe and make it uppercase lest they feel guilty or sacrilegious. Why? It was done for the Creator, and later for the Son; it demonstrates respect for them. Eve those of other religions say Jesus is our brother and the greatest prophet of love and hope. The reason is the parables and the Sermon on the Mount. We all feel He came here to bring hope to everyone and open the way to heaven.

In New York, I met many Muslims through my daughter Carol, and I found them all very friendly. We invited each other to parties, and I gave some of them weekly English lessons. They were all deeply involved in their faith, but they knew well the parables of Jesus, who never carried a conqueror's sword; He won hearts through His love. When I once wrote *he*, they told me to capitalize it; they were sure I had made a mistake. That reconfirmed my desire to learn the right philosophy, not one that came from a religion or a university.

How on heaven or in hell could a book be wanted by the majority of souls? The diversity of minds are more than the grains of sand in the universe, but more humans are uneducated, or just have the bare minimum of education, or just don't bother reading. They ignore fiction, science, philosophy, biography, and so on. They are too busy working to make ends meet and don't concern themselves with spirituality until their senior years. Going to church means nothing if you don't put spirituality ahead of materialism. Your possessions won't follow you to eternity; even your bones will become dust tossed into the winds of time. This is not revelation; it is reality.

My companion (a woman who takes care of me and other seniors who are alone and not interested in sex anymore) wanted to look at the photos I'd taken in the last sixty-eight years, which I have on my computer. She looked at pictures of me as a teenager and said she was amazed at how good looking I was. I ran to the computer astonished; I wanted to see what she was seeing. I looked at my pictures; there I was, nothing special—just another man. I laugh about that now. I'd considered it rude when my wife would refuse to introduce me to women; she'd tell them I was just her husband and drag me away. But God never makes mistakes; I'm eternally grateful to have been created an intelligent soul rather than just a pile of atoms.

Reaching your eighties isn't easy, and even if you do, you're still not sure if you're a genius or a dolt, a saint or a devil. Even Stephen Hawking and his colleagues don't have deep knowledge in any field; all they (and we) can do is scratch on the outside; we cannot get to the core. Hawking stares at photos of space on his computer or in his dreams and sees light so far away that it took millennia to get here and might not be shining anymore; that light is a phantom of God's creation.

He looks up or wakes up and finds himself not nailed to a cross but in his wheelchair; he changes theories as often as I change my underwear. Common sense tell me he's defying the existence of a supreme intelligence due to his physical condition, but he is being tested as millions are; he can choose hope in an afterlife or self-pity without a way out.

He tries to give the impression that he has a great mind and that black holes don't require a super intelligence; he thinks the universe just popped up from nowhere, and God makes no sense to him. But science says there is no effect without a cause; the universe is the effect, and God is the cause. The universe has no brain, but God does. When people ask me when and how God created the universe, I tell them to ask Him but don't tell me.

I met a evangelical pastor who lived in Union City, NJ, when my daughter Carol was a baby. He used to cut through a cemetery at night on foot to his car, and one time, he said he had seen God as a flashing light and had heard His voice. One night, I parked my '55 Chevy alongside his car and went into the cemetery, hoping to be as lucky as the pastor had been.

I had read the Bible but also a lot on science. I found out that the flashing light was coming from the calcium in decomposing bones and the talking was coming from cats fighting each other and a family of raccoons moonlighting. When I told this to the wise pastor, he told me to keep my mouth shut or he would send me to hell. Sometimes, I used to go to his small church for the free breakfast because he never could ask me for a contribution.

Even my doorman knows the whole universe is composed of solid or fluid matter that requires a Master behind it. Every soul knows Hawking is unhappy as a mummy, but he defies the Creator and is paying a high price; he keeps staring at his monitor seeking the darkness of his black holes. If it were not for the Creator, Hawking's black holes could come at any minute and swallow us, defying Lavoisier's reasoning that nothing disappears but changes to another state, as a soul changes to a spirit. I didn't fall for Hawking's godless theories; otherwise, he would be only in his chair and not famous, and I would have kept my Parker 51 pen resting.

We are all in the process of passing away from our material bodies as souls. We are boiling water that is becoming steam—same substance, different form. Sometimes, the simple explanation can penetrate our minds the best and make us happier. The parables are short stories in simple words but built on a rock foundation that can't be washed away by the waves of time.

To say we are souls is logical; our souls remain after our bodies crumble; they become spirits with all the intelligence we had. The electrical energy in our brains is ourselves, and when today's technology stops showing the little ball running on the line at the hospital room monitor, that means we have officially left our existence as humans and are back in a fluid stage as spirits. Our bodies become lifeless because our spirits have left it. Simple explanations cut through the red tape and make everything easier to digest. Does anyone have a better explanation? You have my email.

The Catholic Bible was hard to read until some genius decided to put it in easy words to be digested by the multitude; now, it's popular, and it applies to everything in life. We are all eternal, and after we die, our brains aren't necessary anymore. This confirms that Lavoisier was a man of reason, not a dreamer of theories.

As a teen, I avidly read *Reader's Digest* and loved the fact it was easy to read. Later, I was reading thicker books, but I was also consuming magazines and others media for variety. Religion books are very difficult for the flocks to follow, especially those who aren't college grads, but priests and pastors love to explain such books to the followers; this makes them the chosen ones who lead their flocks.

Sometimes, I question why at my age I'm healthy and doing things a teenager wouldn't dare do. I'm not wrinkled like a turkey, and I've driven accident-free for sixty-six years. My flying records are full of miracles enough for me to be here and write this book. Many times when I was flying on moonless nights, I barely missed what I thought were shadows but turned out to be buildings; I could see people in their beds. One night, I landed on the grass and was grateful it had no deep holes; due to lack of rain, the soil was as hard as rock. After I stopped, I realized that at night, everything is black from above and that if there are no lights in a row, it isn't a runway.

I believe piously in angels; I've been surrounded by them as my life can prove. My hands are perfect—after more surgeries than I can count. I lost four fingers in a meat cutter in Miami. The doctors said I needed a miracle for my shredded hand, and it happened. My time on Earth is getting shorter by the hour, but I take it happily as a mission well accomplished because not many people reach their eighties.

I never heard any fanatic religious senior say "Oh Lord!" in joy for growing old. Aging is automatically our passport to rest in peace. I came a long way to be at my level, but it was worth every minute. I will never say "Alleluia"; I say, "Thank you, my God!"

Some people believe I'm a genius; others are sure I'm stupid. I ask the latter how many books they have read, what religious meetings they have attended, how many languages they speak, how many countries they've visited, and how many books they've read or written. I ask them if they've ever flown in the night and experienced the view of the universe and felt free as an angel on aluminum wings. I tell them I've worked hard for my bread and butter and have been fair to others. I'm eternally grateful to those who helped my dreams come true.

They all bend their heads and hold their tongues, but I break the ice and offer to take them flying so we can get closer to paradise. I even offer to buy the coffee. I tell them we'll defy the owls at a Lincoln Park, NJ, airport open all night for daredevil senior pilots like me. No one has ever taken me up on my offer.

Worse yet are the religious people who read only their sacred books such as the Bible and the Koran and blithely operate on blind faith. Spiritual evolution is a long, rocky, mined road. They still hold on to Adam and Eve's story like stonewalls impervious to attack; it will take them millennia to figure out why we're here. I'd prefer to see Jesus's image in the galaxies than hanging on a cross all bloody.

My consolation is our free will, without which we wouldn't exist as eternal beings with or without our carnal bodies. Proof of this is that we can imagine an afterlife. We can educate ourselves, unlike the animals who end up on our table as sustenance.

If animals had souls and intelligence, no dog would have lifted his leg on the window of Villa delle Fettucine, my gourmet restaurant in New York City, which I opened in 1980. My customers were having dinner, and that dog's call to nature ruined their appetites. That dog next tried to mount a passing female dog. Yes, animals have instinct but not intelligence.

When we face realities such as births, sufferings, and deaths without blind faith, we will understand why life is the way it is and realize our Creator made us the way we are. We have to accept the universe as it is and not challenge Him and accept we are bad. Parents beat their children, family members hate each other, sons and daughters abandon their elderly parents, spouses divorce, and people steal from some and kill others, all in the name of free will. People war against each other and cheat their employees.

When Lavoisier and the children of Marie Antoinette were guillotined during the French Revolution, the multitudes laughed and screamed as if they were in the Roman Colosseum. How many terrorists will we encounter?

Please don't blame the Creator, because He doesn't need to materialize to pay for our sins.

On July 15, 1977, I was thirty-six and living in Manhattan when Princess Mish'hal, the nineteen-year-old niece of the Saudi King, and her twenty-year-old lover, the son of a senior Saudi general, were beheaded in a public square in Saudi Arabia just as it had been done a thousand years ago. It was filmed by a Westerner with a hidden camera. I believe if the Vatican had a sense of justice, pedophiles would have been roasted in Saint Peter's Square daily for centuries now. This barbarism will continue as long we don't change; the law of cause and effect guarantee this. Earth is our hell we created by our free will.

I can face bloody situations; I've played the good Samaritan many times in Brazil and the United States when I've come upon accidents, but I'm a hundred percent against any blood spilling on purpose, especially for religious purposes. Those who inflict death and pain in God's name will never achieve heaven.

God created us ignorant, but today's ignorant ones are tomorrow's wise ones. Tomorrow can also be beyond death. The past is behind us; today is the present, and tomorrow is the present moving on continually. Today becomes the past.

Words cannot describe a beautiful sunset; you have to see it for yourself. You have to listen to a great symphony; you can't just read the score. While I was in Rome in September 2014 to see Pope Francis for few minutes behind the stages (because of my previous book), I discovered marvelous sites of the Roman Empire that were never on my mind; they were no part of my past. How can anyone describe beauty? You have to see it.

I've being in the most famous museums of art in the United States, Europe, and even in the Soviet Union just few years before the Berlin Wall crumbled. I had seen an ad for a special tour of the opera houses and museums of Moscow, Kiev, and Leningrad (today's Saint Petersburg). I was curious and was anxious to see a fantastic, big country with its immense history and technology based on suffering and so much a rival of the United States (only the politicians—not the peoples) but uniting in friendship so the world could become a better place. The total price of the trip was $2,500. I couldn't wait to visit the Hermitage Museum, a beautiful building that housed the country's last dynasty before communism, not the country's people, took over.

We thirteen travelers got to speak to regular people in Russia and were invited to their apartments for tea and fried potatoes; most of them could speak fair English, and they asked us millions of question as I did of them. We asked if they believed in God; they told us the government had closed the churches but not their hearts. Everyone prayed; the law couldn't stop that.

We loved the tour and the friendly people; I knew the end of communism was a question of a few years. As for food, we had enough cabbage, raw bacon, eggs, and tea for a lifetime, but the bread, butter, mashed potatoes, and ice cream were great. The coffee, however, tasted like the chicory they put in it to get more cups out of it.

We couldn't take pictures at the museums, and there were no postcards or books for sale there. I memorized the fantastic paintings by Russian painters as well as famous European painters Peter the Great had bought, but none of the paintings had religious themes. Governments, however, cannot take God from people's minds because the beauty of the universe is God's postcard.

No one can stare up on a cloudless night and not be in ecstasy. I frequently flew my Cessna at fifteen thousand feet at night, but it was hard to convince my wife to come along. She said she wasn't nutty enough to go into darkness and not know where to land because of all the lights below. She did, however, fly with me for about ten minutes, but she said she just wanted to circle the field. We took off from Caldwell, NJ, and headed under a full moon to Bader Field, near Atlantic City, for famous pastrami sandwiches there. We landed thirty-five minutes later. She was speechless as she gazed at the moon and galaxies; she didn't realize how long we had flown or where we had landed.

After that night, she was always ready to fly. She said that she realized why pilots liked flying at night; it gave them a chance to look at God, and that made up for the low salaries and danger. I agreed. I had no choice.

4 The Emerald-Green Light That Saved This Book

I had hurled the first eighty-three pages of this book into the ocean from the deck of a cruise ship because I was distressed about all the negatives and deceptions I had encountered in life. As I was walking to my cabin, I was suddenly in ecstasy; I saw emerald-green light engulfing everything like a spectacular mist in dreamland. I thought that because it was near Christmas, the ship's computer had changed the lights for a few minutes; I expected them to change to red any minute. I passed hundreds of passengers who all seemed normal, but they acted as if I were from a distant galaxy. I ran to the ship's hospital on deck six, where a doctor was chatting with the nurses. I asked him in Portuguese, "Please, doctor, should we talk in Portuguese, English, Spanish, or Italian?"

"Well, young man, English will be fine."

"Doctor, what color are the lights on the ship? This is no joke but a serious question."

They looked at me in amazement. "White, except for the red ones at the emergency exits."

Smiling, I handed him the Italian version of my latest book: *The Big Nest Originated the Big Bang of Stephen Hawking's Black Holes*. He invited me to have a real Italian espresso, and a half hour later, I left. The lights were back to normal. I was happy not because the emerald-green lights hadn't been a stunt but because we're all used to white lights.

I started writing in the dining room onboard the ship at seven o'clock one morning and didn't stand up until six that evening. No one distracted me all day though the buffet lines were busy. On my table were several small dishes and a coffee mug. I was feeding myself like a baby, maybe an emerald-green one. Once again, I had received a message, but this was a spiritual one. We need eyes to see and ears to hear. I like to write surrounded by people because they talk to me and I talk with them and feed my mind on diverse ways of facing life. Writing is like piloting; you might have copilots to help out, but you're ultimately the pilot.

Even travelling as journalist, I could never write cramped up in a room at a hotel; I'd always go to the lobby or the bar to write. Humans weren't created to be alone and bored. The only time I loved being alone was during my night flights; I had to concentrate on the darkness as well as the lights above and below and couldn't afford to be interrupted by someone asking, "Bill, if the engine stops, are we going to die?"

During dinner aboard the *Lirica*, I sat at the wrong table. The nine other passengers demanded I should stay. Smiling at these educated, beautiful people, I accepted. I soon discovered I was meant to be at that table. The grandparents, father, mother, and sisters had taken the cruise in memory of their twenty-two-year-old daughter and sibling who had been the victim of a serial killer. He had assassinated forty-three people in Brasilia, Brazil, mostly young women. The killer was a nice-looking young man who approached women who had no suspicion he wanted to sexually abuse and kill them.

Before they ate, they held hands. I asked if I could join them. They said I looked charismatic, like an angel, when I looked at them. I closed my eyes and felt tears falling. I apologized, but after that, their table became mine for the rest of the cruise.

They all said they felt as if they had died along with their daughter and sister. It took me almost an hour to awaken them to the fact that life must continue. I read my book *In Memory*, about my daughter Carol (1963–96) as she had communicated to me that life was beautiful because we were all God's children. That was the basis for one of my books of consolation.

We became very close on the cruise. I noticed they hadn't received any moral comfort from their religion, anyone else, or any books they had read. When the pain is deep, the only people who can mend broken hearts are those who have traveled in the same wagon and are spiritually deep.

They all cried softly. They said that life was meaningless for them since she had been killed five months earlier. I felt deep sorrow for them. The answer to their sorrow could not be found in our material world but beyond it. We do not associate with the spiritual world because we are too deeply rooted in the material world. But I knew time mercifully heals us; that had happened to me and can happen to everyone. I told the distressed family that their dead relation was sad and was suffering to see them grieve. I said that she couldn't get in touch with them because she was a spirit and that there was a reason for that even if we didn't know what that was.

I had heard my daughter Carol after I, the macho father, had cried for twenty-four hours a day for fifteen days. That upset God enough that He allowed Carol to say a magic sentence to me. It worked; I knew her voice. The main reason Pope Francis saw me for twenty minutes was because of my book *In Memory*; Carol had told me, "Pappy, life is beautiful because we're all God's children." Her words stopped my tears that had started when I saw her body that had been flattened by a twenty-two wheeler in Times Square on the icy-cold morning of February 5, 1996.

I never blamed our Creator for my pain, but I knew there was no cause without an effect or He would be unjust. Behind any individual or mass tragedy is a cause; if not, our material life would be nonsense. We are pro-grammed for a spiritual reason we will learn on the other side, but our good or bad behavior will affect our reward positively or negatively; otherwise, there would be no difference between saints and sinners.

If I had heard God's voice, I could have called that a revelation, but I had heard her voice, which was more convincing than God's voice would have been. I had never heard His, but Carol's voice was affirmative.

If anyone could hear the dead, our lives wouldn't have to be schools for souls to learn to love each other; we would bend our knees and look at the galaxies and know there was a God and it was called reason. When there is no reason, our shells are empty and no nutrients can help us. We'd run around seeking reason from those who say they could talk to and hear God.

Even if we heard God, how would we know it was Him? That's the big question for the majority of us. Even if He showed up as a human, He wouldn't be accepted, and He knows this. Michelangelo was wise enough to please his pope by painting God as a healthy senior with a long, white beard, and it worked; I can't count the number of people I've met who have this image of God.

Imagine if we all could see and hear spirits. Maybe one in a million of us can, but those who scream that God said this or that to them are as lost as those hearing them who go home feeling alone nonetheless. When preachers shout out to the Creator, all they hear are the echoes of their own voices.

When Pope Francis asked me what were the highlights of the Bible for me, I mentioned the parables and the Sermon on the Mount, as they were all humanity needed; they contained our Creator's wisdom that would allow us to evolve as souls and spirits. They can make us as happy as a well-fed baby who burps its contentment. The doors of heaven are not wide but narrow. It feels like I'm the only one who understands the parables are our key to spiritual evolution. For this reason, I heard, "Son, you finally reached me not to beg or cry but as your Creator." I knew it had to be God; Jesus would have said "Brother."

I use my common sense; without it, I'd be in doubt and not happily waiting for my call to the spiritual world. We all must face it happily when the time comes. It's at my door now; I'm eighty-four, not forty-four. Aging is an automatic process we have to accept as a gift.

Some are forced to bend to the guillotine for a variety of reasons, but not all of them had done wrong. We can't know, but the answers will come to us on the other side. Many pay such a price for their wrong behavior; some young Brazilians were executed in Indonesia for cocaine smuggling in 2015—that's cause and effect.

But death is just the passport to the spiritual world, and if you don't know that, I'm sorry; you haven't read enough books based on reason. You haven't read those written centuries ago when angels and demons used to walk on Earth trying to win souls for heaven or hell while God on His throne counted their numbers and was confident that after a lot of suffering, they would all beg for His mercy and would freely request redemption.

I've attended many religious and philosophical meetings and affirm that best I ever heard were conducted by members of the Roman Catholic Church at the Cathedral of Saint Patrick in New York and by speakers at spiritualist reunions based on Allen Kardec's ideas of science and spiritualism in Brazil, France, England, and the United States.

Every religion talks about the spiritual worlds of heaven or hell, but religions are changing; they are admitting that God, Jesus, the prophets, and saints aren't far away in the galaxies but are here performing miracles, healing, and giving advice. Our frustrations with death are lessening as we realize we have a way to avoid hell—hope. Pope Francis has hope as his number-one life preserver.

When Jesus said, "Let the dead bury the dead," He meant we had to not stay mourning at a grave but must live our lives until our time comes. Millions died during World War II, but their families had to carry on for the sake of their children to keep life going until their time came. This is God's plan; we have to rationally realize this in spite of the irrational people who don't. I mourned for my daughter for fifteen days, a long time, until Carol got help from God and spoke to me. That was necessary for me to write books to help the uninformed.

I attended the funeral of the husband of a beautiful, young widow who was completely out of control confronting her loved one's cadaver. No one could say the right words to console her. I whispered a short sentence to her that stopped her lamentation as if I had thrown a bucket of cold water on red-hot charcoal. Everyone died to know what I had said to her, but that's my secret, and I shall keep it for everyone's benefit.

Two weeks after Carol's tragic death, we received a visit from a woman representing the Jersey City Department of Human Resources. She offered emotional therapy for family groups three times a week, and it included coffee and cake. The ambience was perfect for children, and our grandson was only eight. We met several families with children and saw photos of their departed mothers or fathers and even both, and it seemed our grandson began to smile after that. I am eternally grateful to Jersey City and its residents; I found out that the whole country was spiritually merciful and that the good Samaritan prevailed in the name of love.

We have to face our problems just as we face the needle that begins our healing. Not once during those meetings did anyone say a word about religion, but we knew the conversations were based on God's and Jesus's mercy. We felt still connected to our loved ones. I share my experience to give others something to hold on to. In these meetings, Catholics, Muslims, Protestants, and Jews held hands and with closed eyes thanked God for having received our departed ones into His arms.

We will become just spirits the day we leave our human bodies. Spirits can make contact with us because they are part of our world of flesh but are fluid. They are felt and seen by a few of us and indirectly by more people than we can imagine.

Shadows you see and the sounds you hear can make you check to see if your doors are locked and no thieves or rats have entered. Your wife might light a candle for her favorite saint because she may have felt a friendly spirit. More women have contact with spirits than do men because they're more sensitive and have faith that is more solid than men's faith.

How about when a wallet, keys, or a book goes missing? People finally stop looking for it, and that's when the object shows up on top of the TV or on a counter. That happened to me with my glasses; I was forced to buy some new ones, but then I spied my old glasses on the dining room table in plain sight. I laughed and put on put my favorite CD of "Ave Maria." I heard people mumbling loudly in a happy meeting. With my eyes wet with tears, I gave my thanks for the message, and the voices went silent. This has happened to me often; I knew someone from the spiritual world was just giving me a hard time, asking me for a favor, or just having fun.

I used to go to church or spiritual meetings to see if I could make spiritual contact. I'd listen to others talking about hearing God or Jesus, but all I heard were their big mouths. When I was in the privacy of my home, my wishes were fulfilled because no one interfered with my connection to the spiritual, fluid one who had been authorized to contact me.

When I heard the two spiritual messages that changed my life, I was alone. We don't need spotlights and a fifteen-story-tall altar like the one erected for Pope Francis on Copacabana Beach in July of 2013 for the World Youth Day and torn down days later. It cost millions that could have been spent on new schools.

When I heard Carol's message in *Memory*, I was in my apartment on Avenida Atlantica facing the monument, but my soundproof windows stopped me from hearing the Vatican choir of hundreds of cardinals backing up the pope. Three million were at the beach as the country and the world followed on TV as the ninety-feet-high statue of Christ on the top of mountain on the center of the city with open arms looked serenely on all the commotion as if saying, "I forgive you all for eternity."

I heard Carol's voice bringing her consolation to all of us and confirming she was around as a spirit helping us as she did while she was here in an angel's body. At her funeral, more than six thousand mourners paid their respects to a guardian angel.

5 On My Path to Write This Book

To write this book, I had the sense to take a cruise from Rio de Janeiro to Buenos Aires. I wanted to have fun but to write my third book in three years of cruising. I believe it's great to use my pen to express that we are all full of problems in this problematic world due to uncertainty. We don't have any answers to our questions about our final journey to the unknown. No one knows what's beyond the spiritual horizon.

Any idiot can say this or that without reason and then become a famed genius though theories aren't reality and much less reason. Thomas Paine's last book contains his comments about religion, faith, and blind faith; he never mentioned fantasies and theories run on the same tracks.

I love to write in places full of people because they are my inspiration and even my subjects; I can't write away from everyone as if I were in a dark cave or a jungle hut. I was a journalist in my early twenties when I visited the New York Public Library on Fifth Avenue and Forty-Second Street during the cold January of 1955. I was astonished by the building's beauty; it became my favorite place, and I read thousands of books there and took others home. I met some older folks with whom I'd go for coffee. One of them gave me Thomas Paine's *The Rights of Man* and *The Age of Reason*, and my brain clicked. I learned a way to face the world with more spiritual understanding, and I found answers to questions that had me lost. In *The Age of Reason*, Paine wrote,

To my fellow-citizens of the United States of America

I put the following work under your protection. It contains my opinions upon religion. You will do me the justice to remember, that I have always strenuously supported the Right of every Man to his own opinion, however different that opinion might be to mine. He who denies to another this right, makes a slave of himself to his present opinion, because he precludes himself the right of changing it.

The most formidable weapon against errors of every kind is Reason. I have never used any other, and I trust I never shall.

Your affectionate friend and fellow-citizen,

Thomas Paine

Paine's opinion is shared by millions. In *The Rights of Man*, he blasted high society, monarchies, and other forms of government that oppressed their people; you can chain humanity's bodies but not their souls. *The Age of Reason* contained his religious comments, including those on the Vatican. His ideas about Jesus and the parables would work in a religionless world and fit everyone's morals.

Paine paid dearly for his daring writing; his head was being measured for the guillotine by the Vatican though the popes still deny it. He was thrown into the Bastille. A friendly prison guard gave Paine paper and pen, and Paine wrote *The Age of Reason Part I*. Paine had tuberculosis; he was released, and Ben Franklin took him to a farm in Connecticut, where he wrote *The Age of Reason Part II*.

It's very dangerous to play with religion's big names; that's playing with a beehive that can destroy you in the name of the Creator. The word used more than *revelation* is *blasphemy*, the magic word that kept the Inquisition's fires burning and Muslim swords dripping blood. Blasphemy today is the watchword of terrorists who know no boundaries and are sure Allah is involved in their activities, including decapitation. The result is the same: hell is right here on Earth. Just watch the news. Even in Brazil, we can hear shots all night long; these *balas perdidas*, "lost bullets," can make even staying at home unsafe. Jesus's parables could fix this, but it would take an eternity;

that's how long it could take for humanity to evolve spiritually. However, that's our only way out.

I noticed light from Earth reaching the galaxies especially when I was flying at night. I believe it represents souls leaving Earth as Carol's had. But she was chosen to come back as an angel to advise us. The Creator rewards us if we earn it. Begging and pleading won't help us; we must be charitable and loving for that to happen. The omniscient Creator isn't fooled.

It's not necessary to have any special education or have the right ideas to become a writer; I've published extensively, and I've heard many people say they wanted to write a book or were writing one. The problem is not with writing a book but with selling it. Anyone can open a restaurant, but that doesn't mean people will necessarily come to it.

Religion has these same problems; many feel called by God to be pastors and claim to have received revelations. They open storefront churches that not enough attend. Failure is part of our destiny, and it can test our souls. Gold is a temptation, but we pay a spiritual price for it. When we die, all we can take is our soul and the good we've done for others, which God will remember.

A dollar lottery ticket could make us millionaires, but the odds against that are tremendous. I tell young people that if they want wealth, open a business, because then the sky's the limit if they're willing to put in long hours. Some don't like that answer, but we all have our destinies.

When I wrote *God! The Realities of the Creator* aboard the ill-fated *Costa Concordia*, I found out that there are an endless number of books with *God* in the title, so I entitled this one *The Age of Reason*; it's easier to remember and in no way would I be taken as a religious leader. I hope that it will reach those seeking more than religion; I hope it attracts the curious and the hopeful who don't mind digging for wisdom beyond material things.

Bookstores promote books by calling in authors to speak, but at one such event I attended, ghosts must have been occupying the hundred chairs around me. All I could see was the author and myself. No one else had wanted to hear about his grief on the death of his beloved dog, his success in business, and his adventures. But if the subject is a hot one—the adventures of President Clinton and his girlfriend in the White House, for instance— though millions (and I) wouldn't pay a penny for it, billions looking for gossip to relieve their boredom would.

Be careful about spending your money on a book that says we must grow up, marry, have children, plant trees, build houses, and write books before retiring. What moves us to do things not so great in our lives is ego and selfishness; we regret that and end up broke and frustrated.

I pitched the first part of this book into the ocean because I had the feeling I was on the right track but that humanity wasn't. As I tell my grandchildren, "Grandpa Jesus tried to save the word and was crucified. It's time to just enjoy the ride and be together." The green light I saw aboard the ship was God's way of telling me to plant a seed so I could tell Him later, "Well, Lord, I tried just as the saints and prophets did while facing Satan." At the end of this book is my latest hit, "The Message of the Millennium." It will fit everyone's conscience; it's not a religious message but a pure, honest message as we near the end of our material life.

Average people don't bother to learn more because that requires concentration, and that takes them away from the TV, whose comedy shows even do our laughing for us. We rely on our cell phones for social status, and we read magazines to find out what to wear, where to go, and what music to listen to. Churches depend on our tithes, which they use to advertise themselves and the books we need to enter God's house.

I love challenges; I wouldn't have reached age eighty-four if I hadn't. If you don't like challenges, something's missing in your life, and you won't see beyond the nearest horizon. My deceased daughter Carol reached me from beyond and kept me on the road to wisdom and seeking what others with hollow faith didn't care about. My efforts to be kind to others weren't handouts but my own blessings that gave me peace of spirit in my soul. There's no sense in collecting material goods; they won't fit in our coffins.

I drew up designs for thousands of women's sandals, but most of them were stolen at a shoe fair in São Paulo. However, I was unperturbed. I just thought, *My dear Lord, what world did you create?* When I sold our gorgeous apartment in Rio de Janeiro and moved to Miami with only six pieces of luggage, my wife screamed that I was a fool giving away great furnitures, but now, we eat well, travel, and fly around in the Cessna. The memory of a life of good deeds is all we need to face our Creator.

After knee surgery, my wife spent a year in a wheelchair, but she recovered fully. My life is full of miracles; I'm still alive and enjoying oyster breakfasts on the beach, not wanting to burn up later in the day and become a red-skinned creature. God created us different colors to test our prejudices and turn us into moral people who end up happy. It's your privilege to believe or not in God and the spiritual world. I have the right to my beliefs as you do to yours, but I guarantee you I'm not a religious leader selling salvation, but hope.

No one book could ever please everyone; the Bible is purchased the world around, but Muslims and Buddhists save their money on that one. This book's cover explains what it's all about; those who need more than that are blind or mindless. They say, "Who cares? The world's problems aren't mine! I'm concerned only with my family and friends. That's enough!" But the law of cause and effect still applies to them and will follow them into the next life.

I saw a great painting of a serene Jesus staring at the galaxies; I liked it so much more than paintings of Jesus suffering on the cross. The former is the Jesus I have followed all my years; the stench of His blood repels me. I can't face the bloodied Jesus, but the serene Jesus shows us how beautiful life is in any circumstance because we're all God's children. That image gives me comfort especially at my age, when I'm packing up to go.

Roman Catholic clergy can't marry and have children; they won't go through the pain of raising children, go through sickness with them, and pay for their education. They enjoy a comfort that's their reward for being followers of a heaven they ignore and the hell just outside the gates of the Vatican, monasteries, convents, and churches. They don't see the billions of homeless and hungry. How could they ever receive spiritual messages?

I was shocked when Pope Francis declared Roman Catholic clergy account for only about 2 percent of the pedophiles. Though he's against this evil, he gave fuel to the fire with that announcement. I don't trust the clergy with any children much less my grandchildren; behind any altar could be a pedophile disguised just as are the terrorists who call themselves Muslims are.

Years ago, when Carol was a teenager, she bought a little female cat; months later, this loved animal began crying desperately. We ran to the vet, and he told us the cat needed a boyfriend or to be spayed. We felt sorry for the little cat and had her spayed. We finally had peace at home. The cat wasn't to blame; her instincts were natural.

The clergy who give up sex consider that an act of purity in spite of the strong urge to reproduce. The concept of marriage between man and women came from the Roman Catholic Church and was adopted by all the religions institutions as a blessing for families. How then can its clergy forgo their desires to do what comes naturally? Can it be chased away by prayer, or will it be indulged in secretly with other clergy or defenseless children?

When I was a young journalist, I was invited to stay in convents and monasteries at times when I was writing about life behind those walls. I'd enjoy good wine and good dinners and then be invited back to private rooms for more drinks and talk. I succeeded in not ending up as my hosts' desserts. I kept this secret for more than fifty years, but nowadays, I want all the cards on the table.

Those who dedicate their lives to Christ through celibacy should be neutered or castrated to prove to God they're above such temptation. To kneel, kiss fine marble, and listen to hundreds of male voices singing Schubert's "Ave Maria" in the Vatican won't squelch our God-given desire for sex; we're all programmed to reproduce.

Moses was old and physically strong as I am today at age eighty-four as driving, piloting but walking slowly while the young ones mind my luggage's. He claimed the Ten Commandments were God's revelation to him. I offered the eleventh commandment in my book *The Big Nest* that I sent to Pope Francis via FedEx. On another cruise, I wrote *God! The Supreme Intelligence*. My books contain revelation I received as well as some messages that don't qualify as revelation; they're meant to be messages for anyone's spiritual needs.

The mystery of Christ is no longer a mystery for me as I wait for my call to the spiritual world. But lest you think aging has taken a toll on, me, you're wrong. I still have yet to get into a car crash, I still fly, and I swim in the mornings before I write. I feel better than any couch potato. When I write, I mix in different thoughts just as I do when I give speeches to make sure no one dozes off. Maurice Ravel mixed things up in "Bolero" to keep people's attention.

After I bombarded the pope with four letters in different languages within two months, he agreed to meet me for fifteen minutes backstage, no cameras. I was told to scout out on the Internet how to behave in front of the pope—kneeling and bowing and such. Not even God demands kneeling; that demonstrates not just submission but also humiliation. The Catholic Church is losing lambs today as never before because there's a hole in the fence. Churches in Brazil and everywhere are collecting dust, and the Vatican is more of a museum than a cathedral; it attracts art lovers instead of worshippers.

When I met the pope, he was surrounded by cardinals and security. They noticed I wasn't kneeling, but Pope Francis came to my rescue; he explained I was much older than he was. If I'd been forced to kneel, I would have pitched over and someone younger would have had to have picked me up.

In Spanish, he asked me, as I mentioned earlier, what I considered the highlights of the Bible. I told him Jesus's parables and the Sermon on the Mount. Then he made the mistake of asking me what else. I said nothing. He stepped back, and I left. Outside, in Saint Peter's Square on a hot September day, I looked back as if saying good-bye to that show of earthly allure and closed my eyes. I felt Carol's hand touching my face. I heard her say, *I love you Pappy!* That was the highlight of my trip from Rio to Roma. I'd eaten enough pasta for the rest of my life. I dreamed of a good, American prime steak and some famous Brazilian *feijoada*—the national black bean stew.

Even William Shakespeare couldn't have written a book that would have been a bigger seller than the Bible, but most people embrace it and then do what my wife did: put it on a pedestal in the hallway of the house and let it collect dust. I don't mean to blast people's religions or their lack of it as long as they're good people. I've seen families fall apart because someone switched religions. No one should interfere in that matter. Those who are deeply religious want everyone to follow them, but I'm happy with the parables and the Sermon on the Mount. I tell people that, and I'm happy when they accept that, and I end up with new friends.

I am curious person; that's why I became a journalist at age twenty and started putting my nose into everyone's business The more we learn about what's going on, the more we learn that the majority of our terrestrial family doesn't care much about what's going on around us. Those of us who are eager for solutions become hermits because it's not that easy to listen to ball games or otherwise distract ourselves for hours on end.

I flew into a Princeton, New Jersey airport near the university one time, and in the cafeteria there, I talked with some senior professors who had known Einstein. They said that he spoke little, that he felt he had said all had wanted to say. I understood his attitude; when conversations I'm in have no future, I tend to say I'm late, I have to meet someone, and I leave. Sometimes, I try hard to convince myself that average people are too busy to dig deep into our existence in a fleeting world, but most aren't intellectually prepared to face life or anything beyond the visual.

6 On December 6, 2014, I Was Cruising with My Pen

Everyone knows words, but not everyone knows how to put them together in sentences to bring logic to the world, the most challenging job. Ninety-nine percent of the books published yearly just take up space on shelves.

I never had problems creating sentences; I have, however, had difficulty figuring out which sentences are better. We all have different points of view and differing standards; we might have difficulty deciding between chicken or pasta on a flight, but we'll prefer either to a cold, tasteless hotdog on a mushy roll.

As age takes over, we tend to want to show the moral light to others. I've been a journalist, author, and entrepreneur since I was in my twenties, and I was amazed to find out that age attracts others on the same level like a magnet. Wherever I've been lately, whether it's in Brazil or Italy or on a cruise ship, people tap me on the shoulder and ask, "How are you, boy?" I usually stop, smile, and engage in conversation. They're happy to see me walking, not needing a cane or a wheelchair. I wonder if aging prepares us to become like children again as we prepare to move from body to soul as if we were being anesthetized for the long journey back home.

As you age with this book in hand, I believe I'm giving you food for thought. A few years ago, my sister Helen called me from Pennsylvania with news that she was dying at age eighty-two of cancer. I flew in from Rio de Janeiro, and she died four days after I got there. She was down to skin and bones. She said that God was great but that she had never cared for religion, that churches were places only for weddings.

I have a good life; the young usually avoid the elderly, but nature mercifully takes over. Last time I stayed in Boca Raton in a friend's house, I learned about a ballroom for seniors. Men paid fifteen dollars to get in, but women got in for free. The place served coffee, tea, cake, cheese, and fruit. I was surprised to see beautiful women ages sixty-five to ninety in high heels and short skirts and ready to dance all night to a DJ playing Glenn Miller, Benny Goodman, Tommy Dorsey, and Artie Shaw tunes. I became a regular, and I never sat for long. I believe we don't think about death unless were in a funeral home, and even there, it's our human nature to tell stories about the deceased and laugh and joke; life's a comedy according to our spirits.

I carry around a lot of information in my head because I've always been a reader of books, magazines, newspapers, and so on. That includes cookbooks, of which I have many. Unfortunately, most writers are boring; their stories have no color. I think that's why books aren't that popular; they bore people as much as does eating plain pasta, rice and beans, and mashed potatoes without gravy every day. I myself have bought hundreds of books only to trash them because I considered them a waste of energy; they're like conversation with no seasoning. People get right to the point because they don't want to lose their audiences, but boredom is our worst enemy. That's why I listen to classical music as I write.

This book could be my last. I'm not disillusioned, stressed, or worried, however; I'll keep on writing as long as I can hold my pen or tap on a keyboard. I recently had cataract surgery, and I'm sorry I didn't have it years ago. Now, I can see the galaxies even without a telescope and not worry about passing the eye test for my driver's license. I can read and write as well as I could do in my teens; eyesight's a major gift from above.

The fear of coming to a dead end after death scares people; we don't know what we'll find. We say, "He's in a better place" when we stare at someone in a coffin, and we hope we'll be able to adapt when our time comes. We look at each other and wonder who's next. It could be one of our religious leaders who fly all around to tend their flocks. They travel first class, so they'll be the first to hit the ground.

Don't worry about planes; ships sink, buses run off the road, and hearts stop. The trick is to realize that we're spirits here just learning and that our lives, no matter how long they are, are brief. At my age, I'm in a distinct minority. Is that luck? Don't answer! Anyhow, life on Earth is great; it has its ups and downs, but we should always try to perform good deeds small and large.

What Carol spoke to me after her death changed my life and I hope yours too; she consoled me with the thought that life continues. I feel unfilled, however, as I was the only one who heard her besides her and God. What counts is the divine value of the message; others we can safely trash. My revelation in *In Memory* has the power to help others. Its words aren't lost in the wind; they offer eternal consolation.

Though some doubt whether Jesus Christ existed, His parables help us develop spiritually and offer us consolation, He's not a religions icon but a celestial beam of light that guides us.

7 Our Road to Eternity Begins on Earth

E ven children know that the journey anywhere begins with that first step. It took me eighty-four years of steps to realize we need reason and common sense to see what the Creator offers us. My life as a journalist, painter, chef, and pilot has been unique; I haven't followed in others' footsteps.

God's universe is all in color, not black and white, as anyone who has peered through a powerful telescope can tell you. How it all began is the question, not the result, which is right in front of our noses. A few, including me, want to know how it all happened and what it's made of. A few of us also want to know where we'll end up after leaving our bodies. But automatically, sooner or later, I'll get there, and life will go on. We must accept that or become paranoid; we have no choice, but at least we know we're more than a pile of atoms that don't get to eat, enjoy sex, have fun, and wonder about our Creator.

At a supermarket in Miami, I picked up a book with the title *If God Is Love, Why Then Does He Allow Suffering?* I felt an emptiness in my soul at how average people ignore the concepts of free will and the evolution of the soul. I put the book back. Someone nearby asked me my answer to the question the book's title raised, but I just gave him my card and walked away. I didn't want to spoil my dinner with my grandchildren; they were waiting for me to play chef. Cooking is good for the soul.

The more I delve into a subject, the more I feel I've just scratched the surface. I read so much about flying, but something essential was missing. I had to get my pilot's license. I did that when I was sixty-four, and I've made 1,040 landings. Now, when people tell me anything about aviation, I know if they know what they're talking about.

The same thing goes for religion. Many read holy books and attend religious services. I have done that after being invited by others, but a few visits were always sufficient to convince me to analyze religion, life, and death in my own way. I never tried to persuade anyone about religious matters, but I have offered my opinion when I've been asked. Even then, I'd stop if I felt it would jeopardize a friendship.

We know how we're born, but that's as far as our knowledge goes; we are the created, not the Creator, and God won't explain creation to us in any greater detail than He already has. I came to a conclusion (a better word than *theory*; theories have to last millennia) that creation is just a continuation of reality, that the big bang was one of many; they just keep popping like popcorn. It's impossible to put into words the vastness of such thoughts just as it's impossible to put them on a canvas, but attempting to do so is better than nothing.

As I've written, words are at the tip of the pen but sentences are much tougher to create. We all interpret existence in different ways, and it frustrates me not to be able to come up with sentences that can contain my thoughts adequately. We're all after that magic wand that will make our incertitude vanish, and some of us jump from church to church for salvation from spiritual bombs falling.

William Shakespeare's "To be or not to be" focuses on our living and dying. It's as if he had asked, "Does God exist or not?" Sperm and an ovum can create life; this is a phenomenon in that we don't really know how it happens. The word *phenomenon* is used to describe what is extraordinary, what is without explanation or beyond our comprehension. Nonetheless, we exist materially and spiritually in the present. Later, we become spirits, as Carol is now. Her son, Christopher, who was eight when she died, is now twenty-nine. He complains that she's boring him in the wee hours continuously keeping him awake. He's a success, but he realizes the first-class life is so overpriced; the high prices mock those at the top of the ladder who see only gold, not humanity. I think he's following in my footsteps.

If the Creator showed us how He created everything, we'd get too caught up in the blueprints. Let's all just be happy we're not rocks. Wisely, few bother to think about the whole process. At the YMCA in Boca Raton, Florida, was a mother duck with four cute ducklings; they'd all come in from time to time. A sign at the door read: "Please use the side doors when our feathered friends come in for some rest." Everyone loved it; people would take photos as the mother would lead her babes out for some lunch in the grass.

That baby was nowhere before it was born, just like a seed in a flower, but it was ready to grow when conditions were right, as is the case even with new stars. Our souls don't evolve overnight in a microwave; our lives are wonderful from beginning to end. When a baby is born, we smile and are grateful, but when death comes, sorrow and tears dominate the scene. We don't understand that the pain of the loss of a loved one won't last forever and that life will go on. If not, God would be Satan.

Just as Carol needed God's permission to speak to me, all spirits, including devils, can't bust our chops if God doesn't approve. Satan might play the part of a poor spirit being scapegoated by God, but realize there is no cause without effect. No spirits can control our actions on Earth; they can't make us sin or fall; otherwise, that would negate our free will. We have to learn how to love and gain salvation to a better world. We won't need the *Enterprise* to reach beyond Pluto, and besides, our good deeds are all mileage points for the trip.

Those claiming to know what's beyond the spiritual horizon are wrong even if they're popes, voodoo priests, Buddhist monks, senior pastors, and so on. I'll face them in a nice, respectful way, raise my hand in peace, and leave the arena with no comment for them or anyone who pretends to know.

As God's beings, we are born, grow up, learn, work, procreate, plant, and write books all for God's grandeur. I know your next question! How about the bad things so many do—engage in war, theft, and so on? Well, using our common sense and reason, we can see that our good deeds will upgrade us spiritually and that others less deserving will stay behind just like students who fail to make the grade. They will stay on Earth for another hundred years or so to repeat the class. And if they end up destroying Earth, God will create another in which humans again will have free will to evolve or die spiritually.

In Brazil (a country of 220 million souls), even the educated have never heard of Thomas Paine, and very few of them have heard about Stephen Hawking though they have cell phones and computers. Brazilians read on average one book a year while Argentinians read on average eighteen. In the United States maybe one in 10 knows who was Thomas Paine and it include my grandchildren as they learned in the last year of high school.

Even the religious fanatics, whether they're Christian, Muslim, or Buddhist, tell me they don't have time to delve into their religious books— they're too busy working, cleaning, raising kids, and so on. Such excuses keep God's hair white as spiritual evolution goes down the drain; religion is not the only solution promoting hell and heaven. Our Bible collected dust in our house for years until I picked it up and read all eight hundred pages of it in two months during the wee hours. I wanted to educate myself and be able to argue with the unreasonable. I had a million other things to do, but I made time to read it. I want to keep my brain busy; that keeps rust off it. I'll test my thinking in eternity, but I've been self-educated in the Bible and many other matters.

The ignorant say that ghosts who scare living souls are simply illusions, but spirits are around for sure, as those who pay attention know even if they keep it to themselves. I kept my mouth shut about Carol's visit because no one would have believed me. Carol wanted to see me alone; if all spirits showed up to everyone, that would be chaos.

Though some religions make use of statues, Muslims focus on God's essence; they claim He is great and doesn't penetrate our intelligence; He doesn't want His image being distorted in our minds. Those on TV who claim to have had visions or to have been in touch with the deceased are full of BS. Only about one in a million can do that; the others are deceivers. We all see and hear spirits daily, but we ignore them. Someone might stop us to ask for directions, but right after that, they disappear; however, we're too preoccupied to notice that.

I met some good card readers in Brazil; my mother was one. I remember a Cuban woman in Miami who passed away at age ninety-two. Her house was always full of people from all classes of society because she always gave visions that were confirmed on the spot. She wasn't on TV or the subject of books, and she never mentioned money, but people always gave her some to make her life easier. She always reminded us that what was predestined for tomorrow was just a guess because tomorrow wasn't guaranteed by our Creator; He can change it based on our behavior, so all we have is the present. I spoke to her only for a few hours in all of ten years, but I saved her words of wisdom.

The future isn't real because it has no dimension; the only thing real is the present, and our past is a recording of our present. Those who make predictions might be right every once in a while, but that's par for the course due to karma, destiny, and free will.

The cathedral was full for my daughter's funeral in 1996; flowers, tears, and silence filled the structure. She had gone to heaven an angel. The choir sang Schubert's "Ave Maria." A young, tall, and pompously dressed cardinal approached my wife, my grandchildren, and me and sat us near the coffin. He embraced the children and told them not to worry, that Carol was in heaven waiting for us.

My wife gave him a smile that said she would run for his life if she were him. I took him by the arm for a walk behind the immense altar. After that, he evaporated like a drop of water on a hot skillet. My wife couldn't make me tell her what I had said to him. It's still a secret between the cardinal and me. How could he tell us in such a sweet voice to stop grieving? Our daughter, a mother, had died tragically. He wasn't married. He wasn't a parent. He was no authority on heaven or anything else. Not even God could help us. We needed time to heal.

8   The Book That Almost Made Me a Pastor

I wrote *God! The Realities of the Creator*, on the ill-fated *Costa Concordia* off the coast of Brazil in December 2010. Its 232 pages took me seven nights to write. Writing the book put me in high spirits. I had considered writing it a mission.

The book was born on the *Costa Concordia*, which sank two years later, a hundred years after the *Titanic* did. Hollywood was interested in my book, and I talked to eight movie directors at the MGM Grand in Vegas. They all told me they would be in touch.

God had another plan for me, fortunately. If I had gotten rich, I would never have written *The Big Nest* and this book; vanity would have eaten my soul.

Concordia was the most magnificent cruise ship I have ever been on. It was a dazzling-white swan come here from the galaxies to show us how beautiful our world is as it, like a feather, defied gravity. The food was the best I ever had; I had prime rib as rare as I desired, and I had smoked salmon for breakfast. The shows were the tops; everyone applauded and demanded more from the Italian singers. All the *Costa* ships are great, but the *Concordia* is the greatest. My memories of the ship are in my soul and pop out at my and their will. That great white swan was so spiritual that aboard, my words flowed like water from the fountain of heaven.

In just a few days, people knew my name, my books, and my shoes designs. Even the captain would stop at my table for a quick coffee and ask me questions about my life and talk about his responsibilities for so many souls. Believe it or not, I told him *Concordia* would sink soon, but not on his watch. He smacked me in the head and told me to keep my mouth shut. I did.

I believe I would be rich and famous if I had picked up not my pen but tarots cards and opened an office near the UN building in New York. Presidents would have lined up to talk with the "man of God" who had come from above as a card reader.

When I sold my big apartment in Rio and moved to Miami, I knew I was gambling a lot because of my age. But I love Florida, my grandchildren (and now my great-grandchildren), and the clean ocean full of fish. Sunsets there inspire me, and I can wear the shorts, light shirts, and sandals I always wore in Rio. I'm keeping my fancy clothes for my parties in heaven.

I told a young granddaughter about my idea of buying a Ford XLT, a cute, small, but commercial family van that's on this book's wraparound cover. I could drive it around slowly and attract nothing but friendly waves. At Denny's, IHOP, Red Lobster, Panera, or any place I stopped to eat or for coffee, people asked me if I was a pastor. They would ask me about the Bible, even the atheists. I told them I was a spiritual soul, and I gave them answers as best I could. I ended up feeling guilty. I bought a bottle of industrial-strength alcohol for a buck at a Home Depot and wiped off a five-thousand-dollar paint job somewhere near Fort Lauderdale. I feel different now. If I had enough health, I'd buy that van and wrap it in both books. I wouldn't be taken as a holy man, and Stephen Hawking would be my secretary. I would give all the blessings people would ask for but with more experience and spiritual power. My dream is to drive all over the United States and talk to those seeking consolation and answers they don't get from religion leaders at any price. What comes from heaven is free, and it must be given freely. Jesus was not pampered; He preached wherever He was to rich and poor about their physical and spiritual needs because He was dedicated to them, who were sinners with no right to throw the first stone.

Deformity can begin before birth or it can begin afterward at any age. It happens daily to thousands of souls, babies and adults alike. We have the examples of Stephen Hawking and Pope Francis, who has only one lung. The majority of those who suffer in this way come to doubt God's mercy and wonder if He plays favorites. Someone asked Jesus whether the blind man or his parents were responsible for his blindness; Jesus said neither; He said his condition was predestined to bring glory to God. Our reward comes in the spiritual world, the true world, not this temporary world.

Jesus's preaching is common sense, but no one else gave it to us; He is now in everyone's heart. Did Solomon give us any parables that stay in everyone's heart? Please don't email me on this question. One Sunday morning, I received a visit from three nice-looking, well-dressed teenagers who were Jehovah's Witnesses who wanted to say hello in the name of Jesus. I loved it. I was in the mood to give my Sunday sermon, and those stoneheads was going to listen to it.

They were respectful, but I began feeling sorry for them. They didn't give up on their theology, and I didn't give up on mine, which was based on experience, wisdom, common sense, and reason. I told them to say what they wanted to say as I rounded up some breakfast for us.

They tried to save my soul, and I told them about my visit with Pope Francis and my ideas about the parables. We ate my potato pancakes with applesauce; they thought I was from hell. They thought I didn't believe in God. They left like ghosts. Andy, the doorman who had let them in, said he'd do the dishes. I had put aside a few pancakes for him.

I'm always stunned when someone asks me even after all I've said and written if I believe in God; they seem spiritually lost and incapable of thinking logically. I met a university professor at a Boca Raton coffee shop. He looked into my last book for half an hour and asked me if I believed in God and if He had created us in His image. I looked at the happy, intelligent, but reasonless soul and said with a smile, "Yes, you are exactly like God but without His brains." He never said good morning to me again. I could thus enjoy my favorite breakfast: eggs Florentine with béchamel sauce and down-to-earth home fries. Eating is a pleasure even with the restrictions I face late in life about pepper, peanuts, and other edibles whose list grows.

This book could be my last one not because I have a date with the guillotine but because aging takes its toll. I can no longer run ahead of the bullet train.

9 Hope Is the Answer to the Nihilism of Modern Science

When we lose hope, we lose the future. Religions are based on hope; that's why they are the biggest enterprises on Earth. Most of us hold on to a religion, but others treat religion as a long buffet table. Religious people claim that their holy books are shields of truth as they attack members of other religions with words and blame Satan for humanity's bad behavior.

Some places of worship, particularly the Vatican, are materially grand. Splendid cathedrals, synagogues, mosques, and temples seek to help us look beyond our human suffering. But in them, God, the saints, the prophets, and the devil are but ghosts on their altars, and they offer no answers to our questions. Earth is a sick planet, but we can't move to Mars, so we need to save our planet with just our common sense and reason. What bothers me is not the words of uneducated people but the silence of the educated ones.

I never pray just for me; I include as many souls as I can. I don't want to face my Creator as His only Son. I gave parties for which I exercised my culinary skills, but some of my guests turned out to be freeloaders; they never reciprocated or remembered me on holidays. Regardless, we have to help others or our souls won't evolve. Jesus told us to love one another as the Father loved us, but few pay attention to that.

Religious institutions are full of people praying for miracles in return for doing God's will, but they get upset when the miracles don't occur. I was advised several times over the years to put my verbal and mental skills to work by opening a church; people told me just to repeat the words of the Bible and my charm and charisma would allow me to build a religious empire. They said women would fall at my feet in the name of God in my little empire.

I didn't misuse my time by studying to be a doctor; I didn't want to focus on only one subject. I wanted to read as much as I could and learn about many things to stave off boredom. None of my six brothers and sisters went beyond grammar school even though our parents encouraged them to. All they wanted were simple jobs and to enjoy ball games. They called me the lucky one because I didn't have to worry about paying rent or having enough money for food. They were all younger than me; they are all gone, but I can feel their presence.

When I was in Rome in 2014, I couldn't speak Italian though I admired the language's beauty as well as the country. I was there for thirty days, and my knowledge of Spanish and Portuguese allowed me to pick up Italian easily. Learning is a matter of effort, but most people don't want to make that effort.

Those who after reading my books ask me if I believe in God demonstrate they are in doubt about His existence. Our Creator made everything in the universe; what's beyond it is just the complement of His creation. Religion should promote God's mercy, not fear of Him. It should teach us to love and help others; God doesn't need our money. Jesus never had a church; He preached in the open air. He and His believers anchored themselves in God, nothing else, and they were not interested in materialism.

Jesus knew that we would ultimately be blown away by the wind, that every generation would become ghosts whose pasts were recorded in the present time. Why do I mention Jesus Christ in a book that I hope will become a best seller? Why not? Hope is our last wish. Just based on His parables, people can become moral; Christ's message can help humanity in these times as materialism is ruining the Earth and time is running out.

The ignorant ones tell me my time is short and I won't have to worry about tomorrow. I tell them they will face my fate, so they should face the facts and leave the world a better place for their children. I am who I am; I can't change that. My spirit is not just a fiction, and Earth is a school for our spirits that can teach them to love and to exercise common sense; that's the way to heaven. When people face death, their last words are "God!" or "Jesus!" What is relevant will prevail.

I have almost two thousand hours of flying time, and I've taken along people of every religion as well as atheists. I do all the necessary preparation for the flight with a checklist; they all watch to make sure I don't make any mistakes. When we take off, they all bend their heads and pray. The same thing happens when the plane hits a vacuum and we drop a few thousand feet in seconds or turbulence shakes the plane. Their act of praying is what I call Christ's power or God's lessons.

None of us can see what's beyond our noses. We have only hope that life will continue after our bodies perish. I don't mean to give anyone nightmares; all I want to do is let people know that spiritual growth is the medicine we need to live better lives and be ready to transition from body and spirit to spirit alone and to do that gracefully.

Those who run to church in their paranoia leave feeling the same way. The religious blame their weak faith, but the problem is that the paranoid don't find what they seek. Religions say we must have faith. The fact that spirits show up gives us the affirmation we need that life exists beyond death. Why don't we all have the privilege of communing with spirits? I will wait for your answer on that question at williamcanno@gmail.com. I promise to respond to your email quickly; I always find time to respond to those of goodwill. I believe all humanity would lose negativity if we could simply leave our bodies and catch up with boyfriends or girlfriends and go on vacation to a galaxy or Italy.

When you go down into the windowless basement of your neighbor's house looking for your stray cat and the light goes off, every second feels like an eternity. It reminds me of what it must have been like before God created light. We now have the lights of galaxies to keep us eternally happy. Jesus gazed at the universe while Moses focused on just a burning bush, and that made a big difference. Jesus was seeking heaven for all of us while Moses was after bread and water for his people. But Moses received the Ten Commandments for all humanity; they will help us all to live as brothers and sisters. I believe when we hear God's voice, it's actually an angel's voice bringing us God's message; He's the boss; they're His agents.

My email again is williamcanno@gmail.com. Your sincere opinion is very important to me no matter who you are or what you believe. We're all brothers and sisters who have the same Creator. We all have to face what and who we are and find solutions to our problems as well as Earth's problems.

I will not try to persuade you be spiritual in the same way I am. I'm here only to offer hope. Just to think where He got the materials to create the infinite universe is enough food for our brains; we have to bow our heads and thank Him for all these atoms.

10 Provocation—Irritation beyond Control

Suppose you're on safari in Africa and a huge lion jumps in front of your jeep. Your experienced guide tells you that this big male is docile and loves to be photographed. You take a picture with no commotion, but before you walk back to the jeep, you throw a pebble at the lion's nose because it looks stupid and you take another picture. Its four hundred pounds of muscles and five-inch teeth kill you on the spot. Whose fault is that?

It's your fault for throwing the pebble at its sensitive nose. The lion should have realized you weren't there to eat him, so he should have behaved like a pussycat. But a lion is a lion is a lion.

On January 7, 2015, terrorists invaded the offices of *Charlie Hebdo* in Paris, where a famous pornographic caricaturist created a little paper sold at newsstands that satirized and mocked particularly the Muslim and Catholic religions. Even Pope Francis was on the cover of the newspaper holding his genitals covered by bananas. They behaved as impossible children and received a spanking in the form of death. They had tossed a stone at a lion's nose.

That lion was al-Qaida, which is doing enough damage without provocation. This is a good reason for satirists to hold their pencils; they aren't producing anything the rest of the world is anxious to read, and this is not a matter of freedom of speech or the press. Satirists are a bad joke; the majority of people and I don't find their satire amusing; they made fun of others and paid the price. There's no way France can stop al-Qaida and the ghost of Osama Bin Laden; mocking them will only spread their hell.

The magazine staff provoked the lion with a big rock. Imagine the response if someone satirized Jesus by giving Him the face of Satan. Centuries ago, the Catholic Church would have roasted that person at the stake. The magazine staff mocked Muhammad and disrespected the half-billion members of Islam while Europe, America, and Asia laughed. There's no room for such immorality in the universe; it's price will be paid in blood. France learned that mockery is satanic.

This was a matter of cause and effect; we shouldn't satirize anyone. There are so many better things to print. I paint nudes (all my models are in my mind) and receive acclamation for my paintings' beauty, especially in the eyes and noses, but I never do it in mockery.

A satirist with nothing better to do provokes a terrorist for fun. Please, France, don't call this freedom of speech; terrorists aren't stupid. We learn lessons through our suffering. The genius Lavoisier was guillotined before he could give us more of his common sense; his judges gave him the thumbs down in spite of his advances in the field of chemistry.

Religion has nothing to do with such atrocities; radicals on both sides seek anarchy. *Charlie Hebdo*'s offices were destroyed two years before its staffers were killed, but the paper kept throwing stones at the lion; they were behaving like rats in front of a cat. Everything under the stars has its limits, but the Western world didn't notice this. The terrorists had no right to kill anyone; they will face life in prison. Such violent acts can't be tolerated if we want the universe to not become an official hell.

Those who tried dynamiting the World Trade Center in 1993 got not the death penalty but life in prison. Their spirits are condemned to eternal hatred; their souls will not progress. They will have plenty of time to reflect on their wrongdoings while seeing the sun outside barred windows. In prisons, lights are dimmed at eight at night. Prisoners share toilets in their cells and listen to others snore all night. At five thirty in the morning, everyone is up; they don't want to miss coffee. One day is a repeat of the previous day until death comes in its mercy. This is why terrorists would rather die than surrender.

While people debate which religion is the best, blood and tears continue to flow. This will happen until everyone follows the parables, the Sermon on the Mount, and the nectar that can be found in the Koran.

I'm no priest; I want to help everyone hold their swords lest they perish by them, as Christ warned us. I once saw a sign in a Jewish neighborhood in

Florida that read, "Muhammad means peace." I asked a Jewish friend about it, and he said that we all have freedom of speech, that if Muhammad meant peace, we should let it be.

I pity the millions starving in Brazil's *favelas* and other Third World ghettos who have to work up to twelve hours a day, not counting travel time, to earn a pittance. Who cares? I do! It's said that during World War I, Hitler was in an open, flat field and faced an English soldier. He was sure death was staring at him. He closed his eyes and waited for the bullet that didn't come. The English sharpshooter told him something he'd never forget: "Your time isn't now!" Satan had another chance to bring chaos to millions of souls. Imagine if Hitler had died that moment rather than after 240 million had died in World War II before the dove of peace returned. Good always survives evil.

Our beliefs stretch back millennia; we learn things from our parents that they learned from theirs and so on, but they get distorted in the teaching and the learning. That's why the Gospels vary; we don't know which is more accurate after they've been edited and translated over the years. The only things that feel right after all those distortions are Christ's parables and the Sermon on the Mount because they are logical. The same goes for Muhammad and Buddha, whose sayings offer wisdom, peace, and common sense.

I love to write facing my fellow humans because they are the subjects of my books. As I sit somewhere with farmhands or professors, they bombard me with questions. Their differing social statuses don't matter because our enemy is ignorance, but most people have no time to get past their fears and deep into subjects.

Everyone would like to see and hear God, but if He really showed up, no one would believe it unless He gave us the winning moral lottery ticket. Even so, Satan could have disguised himself as God to steal souls. Satan and his devils are always around to be blamed for our mistakes; they try to spoil God's perfect universe, but God doesn't mind because He holds all the cards. That's why he created His sons and daughters and gave them all eternity.

11   Revelation: A Gold, Evangelical Power?

Churches have special members who receive messages and talk directly to God. But there is nothing He can do because we all have free will and can do good or evil. But the law of cause and effect means we have to pay for our transgressions if we want to evolve spiritually.

The Roman Catholic Church has Jesus as its primary contact to God, the Jews have Moses, and the Muslims have Muhammad. Hinduism and Buddhism believe that we must be good in this life to receive paradise or heaven as our reward; otherwise, we will be reincarnated for another lesson.

Jesus told an old priest that he had to be born again to pay for his sins. The old priest asked how that was possible since his mother had died long before that. Jesus replied, "By water and the spirit."

At Carol's funeral in 1996, thousands showed up to pay their respects. I saw over a hundred pair of shoes lined up in the hall; all the Muslims who had come had taken off their shoes because they were in a house of God. This is hope that we will achieve peace and upgrade our moral standard of living. Houses of God are open to all men and women because they were created by Him.

I write about my daughter because she was a great spirit. I don't claim she was a saint or an angel but a spirit that had come here to demonstrate that love was all we needed to live in peace and harmony and establish paradise on Earth. Carol's life and death affected my spiritual writing; she was an angel. Doubting Thomas felt he had to touch Christ's wounds before he could believe. I wouldn't have had to go that far, but I do want proof, not theories.

Many uncharitable people have asked me if Carol's death was a punishment for her and me, but according to Jesus, it was for His glory; He took her as a privilege. We will all eventually die so He can reward us. God uses death for His glory; death isn't the end but the beginning of eternity as we leave our bodies and continue as spirits. It's a blessing to go to the spiritual dimensions at an early age rather than stay here full of wrinkles and gobbling pills. At the funerals of seniors, few tears are shed; people say, "It's about time he went" and head out for a nice dinner.

Seniors are everywhere nowadays, not just in nursing homes. We use common sense to stay out of traffic accidents unlike our younger counterparts. Otherwise, I wouldn't be writing this book.

I'm giving a last look at this book before I send it to iUniverse. Maybe I'm going overboard with my pen, but I'll write anyway. When I'm on a plane at night and the other passengers are sleeping, I feel I'm in a mortuary and feel despair as if I were in the wrong universe. Could it be a fear of flying or subconscious tricks? Once, when I was flying from Miami to New York, we hit a depression, and the plane dropped about five thousand feet in seconds. Everyone screamed, but the pilot leveled off. Everyone relaxed, but I walked up and down, amazed not at the pilot's skill but at my fellow passengers. It was a world of make believe I wanted to leave.

It proves we are spirit; when we die, our spirits will remain. I put on paper what is in my heart. If someone doesn't understand it, there's nothing I can do about that. Our roads to eternity are all different. I rely on positive thinking; the right words help us spiritually. Suffering is part of being human, but the rewards are in the afterlife for those who accept their suffering for God's glory. We don't have to be crucified for God's glory. The Creator will not force us to change; we have to do that.

Revelation is a word that not many understand; people ask me to explain it as if I were a theologian, but I'm just a writer doing a million things to stave off boredom. It doesn't matter what I say; the poor souls feel something in the void. The word *revelation* is applied only to religion; it's something special communicated from God to a man, woman, or child. No one will dispute the Almighty's power to communicate like this if He pleases; He will communicate to some but not others. He gave Moses alone the Ten Commandments, and he gave me the eleventh commandment when I was eighty-three. According to scripture, Moses was a senior; maybe we have to be ripe before we receive revelation.

When revelation to one person gets passed on, it eventually becomes distorted and becomes just rumor people don't feel obliged to believe. Those who are faithful, however, will believe it. Faith and hope stroll around as good friends leaning on each other not to lose balance but to go forward and better the lives of those poor in spirit.

My mother read me the parables when I was eight. She said they would help me in good times and bad. She explained the parables to me and told me we all needed their moral comfort. Years later, when I would come home in the wee hours from my job at a radio station, she'd be waiting for me with coffee and homemade muffins and we'd go through the parables as the rest of the family slept.

We went to church on Sunday to show off our new clothes and to meet friends, boys and girls. I went once a month to keep my social life up to date; I had a big fan club of young girls who tried to get around my mothers' protectiveness; she felt obliged to protect her young baby, as she called me.

God told me, "Son, you finally reached me not to beg or cry but as your Creator." How did I know that was a revelation from God? Very simple. His voice was firm, calm, and balanced. It had to be Him; it was pure reason. I was so pleased that I didn't say a word. It's not the quantity but the quality that counts. Spirits can hear and talk directly to our brains via telepathy. Our thoughts are our conversations, our prayers beamed to the spiritual dimension.

I'd had contact with Him, and after that, nothing more mattered. I had felt Him and knew He was around. Such experiences bless our existence. I don't feel obliged to prove my revelation from God, which I consider a reward, not a handout from Him. I'm not foolish enough to say I saw God, but He did speak a sentence to me that convinced me I was immortal. I know He's around and I'm not alone. He's taking notes in the present time, minding us as we get closer to Him.

Many of you might think that I'm going nuts, that old age took over and I'm once again a child, but my mind is in better shape than it was when I was in my twenties, before I gained logic, common sense, and reason.

I once was worried I would lose the wings of my plane in one bad storm. It took ninety stitches to close up my back after a surgeon had removed a melanoma from my back. I had lost four fingers to a meat cutter at Bill's

Beef House in Miami in 1974. I screamed to the doctors and to God that I needed my fingers to continue as a writer and as a gourmet chef. It took four surgeons two hours to reattach the tiny pieces of bone, flesh, and nail that had been my fingers. They told me the rest was up to God.

The next day, they unwrapped the bandages and said, "It's a miracle!" After that, I had professional butchers handle the cutter, but I told them I wanted them to pray before they turned on the machine, asking our Creator to make us more careful.

Revelations are serious matters; God's name is on them. Carol spoke to me with God's permission when she told me, "Pappy, life is beautiful. It doesn't matter what because we are God's children." And I'm sure it was God who had told me, "Son, you finally reached me not to beg or cry but as your Creator"; no one but God is that philosophical and divine. I'm sure He was referring to the fact that most people who talk to Him do so to get a miracle; they don't contact Him just to say hello.

If someone claims to have received a revelation, that's fine, but we should verify that by reviewing the claimant's life. Did that prompt the person to open a storefront church? The apostles preached outside, not in synagogues or churches or hidden in catacombs for fear of the Romans. The prophet Malachi asked friends and believers for a piece of bread, a place to spend the night, and a mule so he could spread the gospel; he didn't ask for money. Churches ask for a tithe—10 percent from rich and poor alike. It becomes God's money that the church heads can spend anyway they like and their congregations applaud the purchase of beautiful churches, comfortable chairs, and air conditioning. They don't worry about their salvation, nor do they worry about compassion and charity. Years ago, an evangelist leader in New York showed me his collection of ties that had cost him $3,000, and that didn't count his tie clips embedded with precious stones. All of this was in his three-hundred-square-foot closet.

All my writing has the spirit of God, Jesus, and the spirits around us. Their words are like fingerprints by which we can identify them. We know the author by the book and the preacher by the sermon. We should all see *The Shoes of the Fisherman* with Anthony Quinn as a warning. The Vatican could be destroyed by terrorists and scare even the angels. Pope Francis even looks like Anthony Quinn and it could perhaps be a warning from above as it time to change.

When I heard the words *not to beg or cry*, I realized it had to be God; the devil wouldn't have expressed himself that way. I tried to make sense of those words but am still lost. It's like hearing what others consider a great sermon but not being able to grasp its meaning. But God is always in control. The ark was man-made salvation; His is divine and eternal. We are the programmed, not the programmer. Jesus will return, but until then, we must unite to defeat evil.

All the debates on the universe are fascinating. They all mention the universe as illuminated dark matter we are in as fish are in water. Where we are doesn't matter because travel is not related to time. We need time to figure out how long to cook prime rib to medium rare, but otherwise, time is the same everywhere day and night. Tomorrow comes, but that doesn't change the nature of time. Crews aboard submarines can stay below for months at a time and keep time as easily as anyone who has a ten-dollar digital watch.

But if that atomic-powered sub travels at the speed of light to another galaxy, it can come and go, and the crew won't age, because the sailors traveled a certain distance, not a certain time. I heard this theory when I was young, but I wasn't prepared to go against the tide. No matter where you are in the universe, time is the same. If you travel a billion miles in thirty minutes from a Denny's in Pompano Beach and back, I'll still be there and will have aged just those thirty minutes.

If you can arrange my words to give readers a better explanations of my thoughts, please do so; we all seek the star of guidance out of our ignorance. My reward for finishing this book will be a long cruise with no clocks. I'll have fun; I'm tired of racing against time.

What's the next theory of the universe coming up? We are rational but still restricted; we can end up thinking the sky is falling as that chicken thought. It's fine if the universe has limits, but what's the gel that holds everything together? If it's dark matter, is there another type of dark matter that constitutes time or infinity?

Albert Einstein could do anything with time; he could warp it and stretch it. He stuck out his tongue in that famous photo to express his disappointment at being entangled in his theories. The universe is beyond our comprehension, and death will stop us from reaching the unreachable. We are the created, not the Creator. We will fade with the sun.

Einstein is considered the genius of geniuses, but his ideas were just theories, not reality. Gravity, not time, does all the warping and twisting of celestial bodies. But if it weren't for time, there wouldn't be anything at all. Time is the essence of everything. Dark matter is solid; there's no room for space in dark matter. It's a rarified gel we can't feel, but it's there. When you fly, you feel you're floating on nothing, but you're floating on air, which you discover when you hit a vacuum and fall thousands of feet abruptly. That vacuum is actually rarified and much less dense dark matter, but it is as solid as anything else in the universe. Planes lift off the ground when they reach a certain speed and start floating. This is our universe, full of the Creator's greatness and our ingenuity.

God's always in control. He created dark matter even if we don't understand it. He also created light to illuminate the dark matter. Maybe God is dark matter who popped out as God. If God had created light first, He would have had difficulty creating darkness. When I paint, I start with a dark background; that allows me to use color to form what's in my mind. But God is God; we are the chip, not the computer. That's all we really need to know; otherwise, we'd go crazy. We should just sit back and enjoy the show.

My first experience with dark matter was when I flew at fifteen thousand feet over Manhattan on a cold winter night. I felt as if I were leaving Earth and facing eternity. All was beauty and silence. I felt lured into the universe, and that gave me the chills. I pushed the yoke forward, and the plane descended. New York air traffic control told me I had violated its air space by going below eight thousand feet. I replied, "Sir, I am glad I did, because now I feel home." When I landed, I went to my knees and asked God for His forgiveness; I had not been prepared to meet Him.

Einstein mistook the spectrum of light because it could go around an object, especially a spherical planet, but time isn't a spectrum; it's existence itself. Time is the water in an aquarium through which fish swim; it's the dark matter that composes the universe. Our understanding is way ahead of where it used to be; we once thought raw steak was good until someone decided it was better when grilled. Before the big bang, the dark matter was the base, the gel of matter in a fluid state. Soon, I will leave my aged body, but my spirit will always be in the present time; it won't fade into the past like a shadow. Sorry if you want your dog to follow you to eternity; some believe animals have souls, but they are just programmed beings. Let's love them but not go overboard about it. Otherwise, we'd be reluctant to eat chicken and lobster.

Everyone loves to talk about time; science fiction created the idea of time travel, but if we went into the future, that would affect our free will, destinies, karma, and missions; we'd be able to control creation. Nothing would make sense; the universe would be in chaos. Only the present time is valid; tomorrow is the future, and that's not reality. Time is the only existence, and that's in the hands of our Creator; it's not a menace hanging over our heads.

When we die, our spirits will continue in the present time; the atoms of our bodies will go into creating other things in the universe, even maybe a body for someone else. If this is confusing, don't give up; just keep reading and trying to understand God.

When we think of our past, we're not going there but replaying tapes of the past. Meanwhile, God keeps His universal recording continually up to date since Creation. The past is out of reach. Many would like to go back to the past, but that would be as disruptive as going into the future. The past is past. The future is just a hope. The present is the only reality. God's camera is running; the images become a record of the past. Our deeds will determine whether we go to heaven or hell; they will be our eyewitnesses. But don't worry; God loves His creation. We cannot defy God or His plans. If we left the present, our souls would be burned with our bodies.

The 8 mm movies I made when I was a teenager are gone, but I have a few hours of them I transferred to DVDs, and my memory of others is still clear, thank God. Time is a continually rolling tape in the present, the only reality. We can't go to the future; that's a blank tape. We can't go into the past; we have only recordings of that. When we die, we're still on present time, and that's the reason Carol can contact me. Spirits are energy.

We have no choice but to keep living as souls in material bodies until death frees our souls. Life is for us to enjoy as long as we don't hurt others. I came to a peace in my soul and now my wish is to let everyone know we can have hope and exercise our free will so we can evolve and progress. We have only the present time whether we believe in God or not.

I hope you understand all this; be patient, just as I had to when I was training to become a pilot. I kept at it doing the same thing repeatedly until I mastered it. Please don't give up on my notion of time as our existence, or you won't get your wings!

My wife used to play the film *Ghost* after Carol' death; it was a reminder that our spirits will live on. I admired Einstein and his ideas about time, but I hope to meet him, and I hope he doesn't stick out his tongue at me. I have some homemade movies of Carol that I don't play, because I don't want to make my wife or grandchildren sad. When the grandchildren were younger, they'd run to the TV when I played old movies of Carol; they thought she was back. Sometimes, when no one else is home, I play them as a gift from above, but they represent the unreachable past. However, it means we're always together as a family; God has us all on His tape. Carol told me that when love is involved, no one will ever be separated. Only God can rewind a tape, but He can't go into the past to punish our wrongdoings. He can, however, give us a ticket for any violations we've committed.

Wait until you die; God and you will watch your tape. You won't be able to escape your wrongdoings He will have recorded. Einstein said that the differences between the past, the present, and the future are an illusion, but his brain was just a pile of neurons. How could the present be just an illusion? Einstein was mocking us; his theories were just dead ends. Hawking is the same; he said, "For several years now scientists have been aware that time itself is accelerating toward absolute zero, and yet our modern vision of all possible states does not yet include any representation for zero." He also said, "Every time we shake the box, there is a new pattern." When his heart stops, so will his existence. I hope humanity advances in education and becomes disillusioned with these "geniuses" and their lack of common sense or worse yet reason.

As we are so far away from anybody in the dark matter, the only way we could travel the distance is as spirits, but even spirits can't just go racing among the stars doing whatever they want; common sense says so. We are restricted in our human bodies and thus limited. The universe isn't our backyard but a complex set of rules and regulations for everyone's benefit; otherwise, the forces of the universe would be brutal beasts. We will be free as spirits, but Earth will still be under gravity's rules. Geniuses can call the dark matter the universe, give it more dimensions, and dream on just as a wolf howls at the moon, but I and many others will challenge them.

Thomas Edison is a great example of an inventor who worked hard and came up with many great inventions such as the lightbulb but kept a low profile. He wasn't vain; he was too busy. Philosopher David Hume (1711–76) was a big influence on Einstein; Hume didn't think time existed separate from the movements of objects. "It is very possible that without the philosophical studies I would not have arrived at the solution," Einstein wrote. His formula $E = mc^2$, which holds that a fast-moving object appears to have more mass than a slow-moving one, is not logical; it's a dream.

Time has always been a number-one source of debate among geniuses. It's like trying to prove that Bigfoot exists or that God wrote the Ten Commandments; time is a mystery, but we will eventually all become spirits and solve that mystery in accordance with our abilities to understand it. I wonder how those on the other side are facing the facts, not theories, in their new, wonderful reality. Don't be in a hurry to join them; your time will come soon enough, and you will see how silly the geniuses were. We're all mortals impaired by our bodies and will make fools of ourselves with our theories of reality.

Sir Isaac Newton (1642–1727) was referring to gravity when he wrote, "Every object in the universe attracts every other object with a force direct along the line of centers for the two objects that is proportional to the product of their masses and inversely proportional to the square of the sep-aration between the two objects." Newton's law of gravity modified Kepler's (1571–1630) third law, because for every action there is an equal and oppo-site reaction and so on. I don't mean to preach on a subject thousands have written about that still raises questions about our fabulous universe and dark matter; we are the created and cannot jump ahead of the wagon or we'll be run over by it. Newton made many logical contributions to science; he built a telescope. Imagine what he could have done with today's technology. Hats off to those with common sense and rational thought processes.

We need more Newtons to help us stop war, genocide, and other irra-tional behavior and save our planet rather than plan ways to escape it. I'm an aged senior whose days are counted, but I've learned there is no cause without effect.

12   What Is Freedom of Speech?

This is a very important topic because it covers a vast area of behavior. Those accused of saying something wrong immediately appeal to their right of freedom of speech. Religious people, journalists, racists, anarchists, and others use this to cover their wrongs. I hear way too often, "You just offended me! You've violated my rights!" I tell them to sue me. Humanity has a lot of improving to do before happiness will reign on Earth.

The massacre at *Charlie Hebdo* in Paris was perpetrated by terrorists. The tragedy should never have happened even though the country glorified satirists. It was fueled by erroneous moral thinking by people who felt scorned for their religion. I find spiritual beauty in the Koran; it contains less blood, sex, and favoritism; it focuses on love and is meant for those with eyes to see and ears to hear.

Bin Laden stepped in with his guerrillas to free a country from the paws of the Russian bear and became the father of a worldwide terrorist group steeped in blood; it disregards human life in the name of a violent form of Islam. They prey on any soul, and that includes Muslims who don't agree with them. They should receive life in prison with no chance for parole; they should die of natural causes confined to four walls. They have created a bloody theology based on a fictitious God who allows them to kill women and children and think they will achieve paradise that way. They scream "Allah!" as they battle on the front lines.

My daughter had been married to a Muslim, and my wife and I had wonderful opportunities to meet Muslims at parties and dinners. We visited the family of Galil, my son-in-law, in Cairo, and I visited mosques in this country. Galil went to Mass with Carol several times, and she went to a mosque with him and his family. He never talked about religion, but he gave me a copy of the Koran because he knew I was an avid reader with a spiritual side. I asked him dozens of question about Islam, and he gracefully gave me a religious medal that protects Muslim pilots. At Carol's funeral, I put the medal in her coffin along with my heart to help her eternally. I read the Koran with love to see how deep it was, and I found thoughts that would turn anyone's mind to God. Our society will change for the better the day we stop throwing rocks at each other and laughing at comics making mockery of religion.

After the funeral in a Catholic church, where all the Muslims took off their shoes, we went to a mosque with Carol's coffin, which was put on a pedestal under an enormous chandelier. They walked in a circle around it, chanting a prayer to God to help Carol, then a spirit. The ritual lasted fifteen minutes. As we were leaving the temple, I asked for the microphone, and in tears, I said a few words. Everyone clapped. Outside, the temperature was well below freezing; snow and ice covered everything. No one complained. A miracle was happening.

13 Mockery of Religion

The *Satanic Verses*, written by Salman Rushdie and published in 1988, was considered heretical and blasphemous by Muslim leaders. One mullah told Muslims to kill Rushdie because of it. But also in 1988, the new government of Iran said that no longer was Rushdie's head at a premium, but he remains with his neck in a deep hole just like an ostrich. That's cause and effect.

This issue was freedom of expression; it divides the West from the East. No one should be free to insult Muslims or Muhammad; all should respect religions. The French, English, and Germans support freedom of speech, but terrorists will correct what they perceive as insult. Mockery is disrespect; it's bullying. We should respect morality as the basis of a healthy society. Muhammad and Christ would send such terrorists to a perpetual penitentiary as they would pornographers who claim freedom of speech, but I hope my readers will lobby the government to curtail the mockery of tasteless comics who are nothing but bullies.

Many friends of mine have told me to quit trying to save the world, but how can I do that after having heard Martin Luther King say in 1963, "If I knew the world will finish tomorrow I would plant a tree today." I tell my friends, "I would write another article and paint another face." He was killed short of concluding his antiracism campaign, but he was a great man who will always be remembered; those who bring only pain and anarchism will fade into the past.

More than two centuries ago, Thomas Paine faced the wrongness of society without any fear as he expressed the truth or he wouldn't be remembered today. It cost his life at age 72 as he survived with the help of the good people.

As the world became more civilized if I can express this way his name now is on the pedestal of the great names that helped and are helping humanity. As to me no one can prosecuted me now for my truth expressions on my books, especially this one because I don't have the time to offer to predators as all they have is to change realizing that common sense and reason could help them, because earth is running out of steam to a complete halt and is no place to go.

14   Christ's Wisdom and the Unholy Prophets

I wrote this book in 2002; I spent more than eight hundred hours on it at night while listening to classical music in the basement of our house in Weehawken, New Jersey. It contains more than a hundred sections that can be read individually but that cover much of my thinking about God and reality. I never blasphemed anyone not out of a desire to spare my head from the block but to convince people they should embrace the whole world.

I sent copies of my books to religious leaders around the world; the only one to not contact me in response was the Vatican. Some spoke to me for a few minutes and even up to an hour; they said I had much trust in God, but one told me I had been born at the right time; at another time, I might have been burned at the stake or beheaded.

It's interesting that Muslims, even after centuries of frustration and hard work trying to demonstrate to the world their religion was a peaceful one based on love, face terrorists who come in the name of Islam. These terrorists are devils; they have no religion except bloodshed. The only thing we can do is to unite in a positive, spiritual world and keep our eyes open; they don't have God to back them up.

Terrorism comes disguised in a million ways; one of them can be as a scientist who tries to deprive us of hope in an afterlife. Terrorists can use brutal force, but they cannot kill our hopes of an afterlife unless we let them. They use their religion to get soldiers to wreak havoc on our planet.

We all know death is part of living; death is a necessity because our bodies deteriorate; we cannot stay forever on Earth because it's not prepared for perpetual carnal existence. To live for a thousand years would be torture; boredom would take over, and we'd commit suicide. I was a suicide hotline volunteer in New York years ago, mostly in the wee hours, mostly around Christmas time. I leaned that the main problem was boredom. Few had health problems; most were lonely due to divorce, death of companions, and so on. That was interesting; I was always too busy reading, learning, and opening the universe's doors to be bored. But I couldn't force anyone to read; the majority didn't care for that, nor did they care for cooking, painting, flying, or anything else that would have kept them busy.

I learned to fly at a late age, and I always loved to write and cook. My advice is to keep active; cut the grass and pick the weeds and you'll never know you're aging. Watch good TV shows and travel as much as you can. Duck out of movies you don't like; get a cup of coffee instead.

15 Terrorism Dominates Brazil

When Osama Bin Laden was killed, everyone knew it wasn't the end of terrorism, which spreads like the plague. Terrorism can appear in politics, religion, and racial discrimination; terrorists keep shooting until they generate great fear among the populations in which they operate even in small numbers. People wonder who will be the next victims; heavy artillery, tanks, planes, and submarines cannot counter terrorism; only angels can.

Those terrorists who call themselves Muslims are counterfeits who harm their own people. They are evil; they do not value their lives or their families. They are a challenge to humanity as a whole, and to stop them is everyone's task. We have to fight Satan disguised as terrorists before it's too late. If it weren't for the Americans who died fighting the Third Reich and the Rising Sun, we'd be living under fascist ideologies. I remember gas and sugar ration cards in the States, but it was worse in England.

America's interventions in the Middle East are necessary to prevent World War III, which could end human life on Earth. But other countries just sit and wait. This book is not meant to be a history lesson; bookstores are full of those. I just want peace to prevail, but this is something we all must learn to do on our own; no one can do it for us.

The cowardly attacks of September 11, 2001, were the beginning of every country's attack on terrorism, but only the United States stayed on Bin Laden's heels. Now, there are angry individuals who are ready to blow themselves up due to their negativity. Terrorists have no particular ideology; they follow any path to atrocity. It took an army in Paris to hunt down the three killers, but sooner or later, evil will come to light.

Brazil, where I lived for twenty years, is as poor as India; people there work hard only to bring home rice and beans to their homes in the favelas that not so long ago were the homes of slaves. Their neighborhoods aren't safe; bandits lurk in the dark. Those who immigrate from other Portuguese-speaking countries are no better off than they were at home. The terrorists there are those who rob and kill others—men, women, and children alike— and people are afraid to identify the terrorists. Brazil has few jobs to offer, and immigrants become street peddlers of stolen merchandise and live on contaminated food and water. The country is definitely Third World.

The Brazilian courts are slow and discriminatory in every aspect; the politicians are corrupt, and the county bows to the anarchy created by terrorists. Better-off Brazilians turn a blind eye to those on the streets, but the law of cause and effect applies here as well. Man-made calamities are as deadly as natural catastrophes. So many Brazilians want to flee their country, which they think is going downhill rapidly. Others can't even dream of leaving because they can't afford it; their money goes for bread rather than airplane tickets.

Migrants still come to the country through its porous borders, and some are sponsored by al-Qaida. They would like to take over a country so close to the United States and bring on Armageddon. The problem exists today.

Brazil is poor in technology and skilled labor, but the world needs its soy, corn, fish, and coffee. The Amazon basin is being destroyed to raise meat for export. I hope it's just a nightmare, not reality, but I won't be around to see it. I can only warn the world; the rest is up to all people of every color, God's family.

The prison population in Brazil is over 80 percent black; they are not imprisoned for long because there is no money for prisons, but there is also no money to educate them, so they return to lives of crime. The government tells its citizens to hand over their money to robbers; it's better than getting killed. Image a land as big as Brazil in the hands of terrorists who want to dominate the planet; no one could stop them; Brazil's people would be held hostage.

I was having breakfast in Jersey City when the planes hit the World Trade Center; I'm afraid the same could happen in Brazil. Gangs of black and white youths frequently stage hit-and-run robberies. I was in a restaurant in Rio when five black and four white teenagers came in asking for handouts. The staff quickly served them sandwiches and cans of Coke. I asked the owner why he didn't call the four police officers on the corner; he said it would mean the end of his business.

In 2014, 108 crosses adorned the graves of that many police officers as politicians earned a hundred times the minimum wage. Police officers can't afford even bicycles. The teenagers there live in poverty right behind luxury condos. They are minors, and no one can put a finger on them until they are eighteen. One young killer was released because it was the day before his eighteenth birthday. He was sent to an institution for minors for twenty-four hours. He was released. Months later, he was jailed for another murder, but he will be out soon because of prison overcrowding.

Brazil is a brewing pot for terrorists. It's a beautiful country, but muggings there can be fatal. I was born in Belo Horizonte and became a journalist at age twenty. I spoke with Brazilian friends about writing this book; they told me to worry about my bread and butter and just write dime novels; there's always a market for those. Too many don't care about whose dying—criminals or police—as long as the beer is cold and the ball game is on. Life can be a paradise if you have enough money, but I wonder what will happen when doomsday approaches and the crying begins.

I remember living through a blackout on the East Coast in 1965. I looked across the Hudson toward New York and saw total darkness. The blackout affected people from Ontario to New Jersey; thirty million people in eighty thousand square miles had no electricity for up to thirteen hours. It was all due to human error; a few employees made some wrong moves. Back then, the word *terrorist* wasn't in the dictionary, but this is something terrorists could do, and it could last for months if they blew up whole power plants. They could do the same thing with the water supply.

We humans must learn to love each other and live in peace or face the harsh consequences. I was thirteen and living in Brazil when World War II ended. The carnage didn't cross our frontiers, but we could smell the stench across the ocean. One of my uncles died at Monte Cassino in Italy. But today's wars have no frontiers; a few terrorists can strike anywhere and kill many; they have no concern because they believe they will end up in paradise one way or another. Pearl Harbor and 9/11 could happen again. Syria and Iraq are on the hands of Bin Laden's followers, and they're spreading their brand of terrorism; terrorists are popping up everywhere like popcorn. They are not rational people by any stretch of the imagination. They always seem to attract enough volunteers for their cause who are willing to kill and be killed for their ideology.

The world knows how Brazil's laws aren't tough on crime, especially crimes involving drugs. Cocaine traffickers get out after two or three years, and all the while they're in prison, the conduct business as usual on their cell phones. It doesn't take much money to bribe prison guards whose salaries are barely enough for rice and beans for their families.

One Brazilian was arrested in Jakarta, Indonesia. He had flown there to supposedly give flying lessons, but the tubing in the wings of his hang-gliding (asa-delta in Portuguese) held thirteen kilos of cocaine. Another Brazilian was found in Indonesia with several kilos of cocaine in his surfboard. They were both executed by firing squad this year.

Brazil is a stewpot of drugs and terrorism. Its politicians skim millions of dollars for themselves. Brazilians are more negative about their country than Indians are about theirs. President Dilma Rousset, now in her second term, asked the president of Indonesia to send the two Brazilians back to spend time in jail there, but that was refused. Indonesia sent back their ashes. She wanted clemency for them, but she ignores the needs of a country begging for clean water and an environment free of pollution all while treating drug criminals as minor inconveniences in Brazilian society. Dilma represents the pandemonium in Brazil; the country will be easy prey for terrorists because of its extreme poverty and the hopelessness of life there for millions.

I remember seeing hundreds of shoeless and shirtless children racing through the beach at Copacabana and grabbing purses, cell phones, beach towels—anything they could get their hands on; no bathers confronted them, nor did the police; they are afraid of provoking the masses of poor in the country. The retaliation they would face would be deadly. When the police go into the favelas, they face gunfire and blockades that even tanks can't get through. Any police helicopters come under fire as well. Well-to-do Brazilians ignore these realities as they bake on the beaches where the water is polluted by human waste and they contract melanoma by the thousands. And I'm much too old to protect Brazilians from themselves.

I knew a family man who brought hundreds of kilos of cocaine from

Uruguay to Rio and made a fortune; he was living the good life until he was arrested. He was sentenced to fourteen years in prison but spent only two there. He had "found" religion in jail, but as soon as he was out, he "lost" his religion. He's free as bird now, having paid his debt to society. He still owns the businesses he bought with his drug money, of course. He and his type and even the politicians laugh at Brazilian law. How in heaven's name can Dilma say she represents such a huge, impoverished country? Syria and North Korea are examples of what can happen when the people in charge get there not on ability but by being put in their positions by idiots.

I'm writing this much about Brazil because if it goes to the terrorists, the war the United States might have to fight could make the Vietnam War look like a piece of cake. They way out of this mess is through reason and education. In spite of what I have written about Brazil, I don't think it's a lost cause. I think what we are hearing are cries for help of a fellow nation on Earth and at United States back yard.

Abu Bakr-Baghdad used religion to spread his hate with a mind more abnormal than Hitler's. He is one who has made our life on Earth a real spiritual challenge; why does the Creator allow this to happen? Hitler didn't use God to back him up; he didn't even mention the Creator; no preachers were his targets. Now, even more evil is being unleashed as Abu decapitates people in front of TV cameras. I believe women and children will be also on his diabolical list. Syrian and Iraqi soldiers have to fight or face decapitation. Imagine if the whole Muslim world accepts this new evil; there will be no place to hide. The solution will come when Christians, Muslims, Buddhists, and all the religions on Earth hold hands in the name of our Creator, who gave us free will, intelligence, and common sense. God gave us the rights to stop evil as it is necessary when reason and common sense are not accepted by outlaws.

Mecca and the Vatican have all the ingredients necessary to face the cancer left by Bin Laden and win the moral battle; if they don't, they will bring chaos never dreamed of. Hate, immorality, disrespect, and mockery can bring down empires, and Earth is in the process now of breaking down; it lacks enough freshwater, clean air, and food for us earthlings. Could this be a punishment from the Creator? If you could prove otherwise, you'd be our next guru!

16   Earth Is Our Mother

We are the only living creatures that can look at the galaxies and wonder how they came to be and what or who is behind it. But we are not geniuses; we hit mental stonewalls on the subject. We don't really create anything; we just mix cement, sand, stone, and water to come up with concrete; we can put together flour and yeast and water to make bread. But all these materials are merciful handouts from our Creator, who made everything. We can procreate, but we cannot create. Who's behind the universe itself? Our common sense tells us someone had to create the light by which we see everything. Let's be thankful for the material we have at our disposal; our Creator is using Hawking to test us all.

I am getting exhausted reading about all the supposedly great men and women who are great because others say so. I fake illness when I listen to people pontificating about our thoughts and behaviors and hike around the block. I come back when they are wrapping up their BS about how they can help lost souls. These are generally people who have never had children keeping them awake at night or spouses who cause them problems, but they still charge $300 per hour to listen to others' problems. I have a forty-year-old niece with an office in Washington, DC, who is very busy saying what I don't want to hear or pay for. Sometimes, I believe our world is full of suffering as well as comedy.

Earth is a stage, and we are all performers on it; some create beauty while others create mockery while the masses applaud. We will learn our fates after we become only spirits, so we better have insurance policies of good deeds. Our Creator will not punish us eternally, however; those of us who don't make the grade will come back for more classes in another life.

Mine are just theories, but they are based on reason. God doesn't jump out at us, but we can sense Him when our consciences bother us; we can feel His eyes glaring at us and His camera rolling.

I used to be stressed when I'd hear people talk about God, Allah, Jesus, Muhammad, Buddha, Moses, Abraham, and other religious people, but as I aged, I mellowed to the point of loving it. Image the wars that would still be raging if we didn't have people of faith.

The universe in its totality is not intelligent; it just offers us ways to go, just as the sun offers a baby turtle a path to the sea. It's programmed that way; it instinctively follows the commands of its Creator. Instinct isn't intelligence, but it can help us avoid getting hit by a car and tell us when we need to eat and take our next breath. That's the handiwork of our Creator, who came up with stars and dark matter alike. Without His supreme intelligence, gravity wouldn't work and the planets wouldn't exist. How does His intelligence work? Ask Him and then tell me! But I know the answer; I can whisper it into your ear or tell you in an email, but let's keep it our secret.

Did anyone ever ask why Earth spins around every twenty-four hours with no need for fuel or maintenance? I have, but the answer is not in this book because no earthlings would understand. When someone asks me where I came from, I just point to my Galaxy XLT and hop in it and drive off because I don't want to spoil my day. It's a made in America white-XLT-FORD EXPLORER-2015 and heavy enough to keep the bad drivers away as I am driving for 67-years accident free and the same goes to flying.

17 Einstein: A Genius or Just a Theoretician?

I still stare at the stars; my imagination has never had a day off. I wonder why we are here, why life is so strange, why we are so frail, why we have no guarantees, and why we're materially restricted. But I'm not alone in my questions.

I was only twenty-one but a professional journalist when I interviewed an old Catholic priest in a ghetto. He loved to feed poor children. He opened his heart to me; he said I gave him the confidence he needed to express his feelings about our Creator. He told me to put down my pen because I'd never forget what he was going to tell me. He affirmed we most keep active our memory as it is forever.

Time is the only real dimension, but I can play back my memories just like watching a movie because our memories are huge banks of information about the past better than any computer and can run for a hundred years. Our memories are in our brain, in which we have a type of computer chip called our spirit. All my books are in mine, along with twenty thousand color pictures. I hope I'm giving you some food for the thought because sooner than later, I'll be far away and facing dimensions few people dreamed off, but it's all in this book for those seeking more than one sugar or two!

Because I had been on Hawking's heels, a friend pleaded with me to analyze Einstein as well. I flew to New Jersey one afternoon and met some old professors who had known Einstein when he was at Princeton University. They told me he didn't like it when people would say he didn't believe in God. The more I read about him, the more I realized he had felt he was in the presence of a great power.

I'm not a biographer; it's not my line, and I like a 360-degree view of life, not a narrow one. I have learned a lot from others, but I have my own way of seeing the universe and God, and I have free will to do so. I don't follow others' reasoning without doing a lot of digesting of it first and rereading Thomas Paine's *The Right of Man* and the *Age of Reason*, which I first read in my youth.

As far I know, Einstein didn't patent any inventions, but he opened the doors with his calculations and theories. He had a tough life; he came to the United States just prior to the tragedy of World War II and offered his talents to all humanity.

I have the right to my opinions as everyone else does; I could right now be at a friend's house in a group eating, drinking, and listening to nonsense, but I choose to think about matters that I consider important. Our choices in any aspect of life make it a colorful rainbow, a buffet of everything from the religion we choose, the spices we like, and the friends we make to the spouses we ask to marry us. We're all divided along professional, religious, and personal lines because of different theories and ideas we hold. That's fine as long as our beliefs keep us happy and don't hurt others.

Einstein could do anything with time; he turned it into a big web that holds everything. I have an image of a spaceship passing Earth, which is sunk into the web. The image reminds me that 99.99 percent of theories can decorate our daily vision of how interesting are our human minds, particularly those that haven't lost contact with our childhood minds. Time could be the dark matter and everything could be a part of that. We don't know time's DNA, but we can agree that time was here even before the universe was, and the idea of the big bang confirms this. Those with common sense don't put their lives on the line for any theory, but my idea of time is not based on fantasy; rather, it's based on logic.

Einstein used to say he followed his intuition or perception because the universe was always in motion. That's all fine, but it doesn't have anything to do with present time being the only dimension. The past is history, and the future is but a dream. I can contact Carol because she is a spirit. National Geographic and Discovery channels have a great collection of tapes based on history; they bring to us in the present time what we might have otherwise forgotten. They confirm our past even as we exist in the present. Imagine God's perfect records on everyone and everything in His creation. Others disagree with me because I'm not a famous scientist, but God's computer files are eternal.

We are always in the present; we aren't ping-pong balls bouncing around. This was a concept I entertained when I was young, but others thought it was nonsense. If you're one of them, don't email me; I can't send you common sense.

God has His tapes to keep control over His dominion continually; He never sleeps because spirits don't need to. People ask me where I get my imaginations, and I tell them by seeking logic in our perfect universe. My ideas could be idiotic dreams no different from those of professors or muleteers, but we won't know until we get closer to more wisdom or eternity. In the meantime, let's all act not as fools but as those who seek logic and understanding.

Einstein said he needed 90 percent perspiration and 10 percent inspiration; nothing comes easily. But too many of us think that the ideas that pop up in our minds are all insights from God and we jump on the wrong wagons. I'd be happy to suffer 99 percent perspiration if that meant I could enjoy 1 percent inspiration. I'd be able to make clouds stop right over reservoirs to fill them with rain or a car that runs on atomic fuel, but our scientists think it's more important to reach Pluto than to solve our problems on Earth.

Many people want to open a string of coffee shops and become as rich as Howard Johnson, but many sink their money into entrepreneurial endeavors and lose their shirts. They think action can take the place of thought. The limited don't see the unlimited realities as they are because they are limited by their capacities. The unlimited realities appear even in any limited realities.

18   Abraham, Moses, Jesus, and Muhammad

Let's take the fanatic, ignorant veil from our consciences and intelligently compare the great names in religion, because they affect everyone, even those who aren't religious.

What was written about those prophets was changed according to writers' beliefs or lack of them over time. These prophets affect the majority of us as souls spiritually lost and not at peace in the labyrinth of earthly life. But no one can deny there is just one God.

The feeling of incertitude about the past causes most of us to shut down our common sense when it comes to dealing with these prophets. Their original thoughts have been distorted over time and are still subject to further distortion today, so how can we follow them? A few impose on the multitudes what they believe these prophets' original teachings were; the teachers rely on the lack of vision among the multitudes, the majority of whom aren't professors of religion or even college grads. They just follow the dictates of the preachers and hope for the best until they fall into the abyss of suffering.

Let's begin with Abraham; his preaching affected two who followed in his footsteps. Let's forget about Adam and Eve, whose story is a fable. They gave us all "sinners'" passports even before we were born. Adam wasn't wearing his pants when Eve persuaded him to sin. Since then, he has taken revenge not against God, because he is a mightier, but against Eve, because she is weaker. Nonetheless, loaded with female wisdom, she kept Adam in line by making him sleep in the guest room for few nights.

What a beginning! Fortunately, this mud man is not considered a prophet but the biggest, number-one sinner in the Universe mainly because he was the only man around then. Eve is number two. They are roasting in hell (purgatory was created much later, around 1400, by the Vatican) because there was no religion around then and he had no money to pay any tithes. Adam had been a sucker for Eve, and unethical discrimination against women continues to this day; revenge takes a long time to be eliminated from guilty consciences.

Adam was more responsible for accepting the apple than Eve was because we can say no with free will. The problem was that Adam was in love with Eve, and being in love unbalances us. Eve, in her *au natural* state (just look at the paintings of her in the Vatican museum), could have gotten Adam to eat two apples.

Who then was Abraham? Again, a figure of mythology but one that helps us grasp reality and become spiritual beings in the midst of our suffering. The following line of prophets (with the exception of Christ) followed the pattern of Abraham because he pleased the multitudes, who weren't spiritually balanced. Abraham embraced all souls with unconditional love. His sayings, small histories now called parables, are easy to digest, and they keep us from doing evil.

Everyone loves winners; Jesus looks like a loser because of His death on the cross. He behaved like a lamb and died for us. This is why many of us not on a higher level of spirituality keep His body on the cross as a human lamb but ignore His wisdom. They see the capitulation of the body, not the triumph of the spirit. Abraham and the others would have used their swords rather than succumb to a real cross, but they succumbed to the invisible, heavy cross we all carry. Christ said, "Follow me because my cross is lighter."

Jesus is in history to stay, while others come up only sporadically because they never begged to help us in our moments of drinking from the cup of bitterness and facing death. However, Jesus will be with us when we scream our last word, "Jesus!" My son-in-law, a devoted Muslim, and I screamed to Christ for consolation when we faced our chalice of bitterness in front of Carol's body; he didn't think about other prophets. When he saw his wife's body in the morgue, he fell to his knees and screamed, "Jesus, please help us to get through this pain!"

I embraced him, trying to wrap his pain in mine. I told him Carol was living as a spirit again. In my spiritual experience, that moment was the maximum of the power of the preaching of the One who died to live and give.

Abraham

Abraham is the father of three faiths. I'm sorry we still search for answers to the whys of life through science, philosophy, and religion and their illogical theories. Abraham's time on Earth is so illusionary that no one can prove he existed. Moses, Jesus, and Muhammad are well known without the image of an altar to sacrifice their sons to a God who demanded blood sacrifice and at the last second changed His mind. That's the image of a Viking blood god.

Abraham was a womanizer; some claim he was a feminist, but in his days, women were just plain slaves and toys until Jesus came to change this unmerciful thinking. He gave hearts to the heartless when it came to how they treated the "weaker" sex—their concubines and mistresses. But this attitude still reigns today in certain Arabic countries and among certain aborigines. Today, women's lives are better, but this is a still just a historical blip subject to reversal according to men's convenience.

Some believe God created a physically strong human being called a male and a weak human being called a female to please the male, an inferior animal; we have prisons to reeducate them, however. Today, the sexes are unequal due to ignorance of moral laws. I don't know if in Abraham's time women were subjected to the barbarian, inhuman cutting of the clitoris to keep them from enjoying sex, but the practice of female circumcision was to keep them sexually "neutral" and faithful to their spouses. They could not experience the joy of sex and the way it binds humans in marriage.

This bond is cut off with this cruel, evil act, and no love can be generated by it. I would begin a crusade to stop this irrational, perverse act, but no religion would back me up because love is involved and no money would come from it. This act is not mentioned in any written books; it was passed along faithfully to all generations. Even today, thousands of young girls are still suffering this evil procedure by Islamic radicals to "protect their honor"; nothing is being done to stop this act of wanton cruelty perpetrated on the defenseless. Those men who believe women are inferior to them because they came from Adam's rib must remember that Adam came from mud according to dopey, satanic mythology.

I believe if "castration" is necessary, it should be practiced on Catholic priests and nuns who have taken vows of celibacy anyway. This would remove the temptation of pedophilia. Those who practice pedophilia should be sentenced to life in prison, after which they will suffer God's punishment.

If circumcised women refused to have children (the most crucial job on the planet) because it was too painful, in a hundred years, humanity would cease to exist. At bedtime, the lion becomes a lamb seeking affection that he did not give during the daytime but irrationally believes he is entitled to it. I believe religion was created by men for men, not women, who are still so rare in the pulpit. All the prophets (except Jesus Christ) were violent, macho men; Solomon had a bedroom the size of a football stadium to accommodate his harem, and people had to pay for it or face the sword.

If religion had been touched by women, it would be humanized and bloodless (no burnings at the stake and no holy wars) and free of pedophilia. I agree with France: *Vive la différence* when women are concerned.

Abraham's myth is the right one for those seeking material convenience; Abraham was the first to preach about surrendering to this merciful and feared God while he was slaying his enemies and using women for his pleasure; he was willing to sacrifice his own son. He appeals to those with little spiritual sense but offers no logical way of living. The basis was there, but it needed to evolve a lot; it was not according to the Christ's conception of God and justice. The Koran says that men are equal to women but that men can have four wives; women can be stoned to death even by their families for looking at a man. Arabian laws do not approve it; they hold that this unmerciful act is no longer in practice, but we all know it is not absolutely true.

In September 2014, I met a young, beautiful, Arabian couple on a train going from Rome to Milan. I am a charismatic senior in my eighties, and they admired my book *The Big Nest*, which he wanted to buy. We talked for over three hours; he invited me to visit them if I was ever in their country, and he gave me his business card.

While drinking coffee with them at the train station, I noted that his young wife was very happy with her life. She touched my hand with an angel's affection, but that caused him to hit her hand and slap her face. Her tears of pain and disappointment cascaded down her cheeks. I rose, glared at him, and told him he was not a normal human being. I ripped his card in two and tossed it at his face. I told him he did not deserve such a nice, beautiful woman. I called over three policemen and explained that he was beating his wife.

He tried to talk to me, but I couldn't face him; his act was unforgiveable, pure, macho barbarism. How could he face her and tell her he loved her?

Such machismo has come down the generations, father to son, while mothers and daughters have to accept it with no help from God. They feel inferior; they can give birth but lack the muscle to repel the devilish, macho nature of men.

Even today, some Muslims in Saudi Arabian are trying to reinstitute barbaric punishments such as chopping off the hands of thieves, stoning adulterers, etc., because they do not know Christ's wisdom and love. As a result, blood spills, and it could be anyone's blood because of cause and effect. I don't condemn all the men of any particular country, just the bad apples.

Ignorance predominates as it did at the beginning of society, and I wonder if I deserve to come back again as an angel to help the evolution of our brothers and sisters, but it is not my decision or yours. I am not alone; a minority is working hard in the field of morality, which I consider the most difficult task for us.

Moses

Moses, the second prophet in line, also preached violence about God, reflecting the barbarian stage of humanity at the time, but the Ten Commandments, his number-one message from the spiritual world, was a moral track for people to follow then, and it still is today. At the end of this book is my eleventh commandment that complements Moses's ten, and I know everyone will agreed on it, because good ideas don't come as mistakes.

His "eye for an eye" justice was better understood by people of his time; they were more barbaric than people are today, and they didn't understand love. Moses couldn't express himself more spirituality because only a few would understand him, but he left a base for Jesus to anchor onto.

There are two distinct parts to Mosaic Law: The Ten Commandments and the civil or disciplinary laws increased by Moses and God. The first is invariable;

the second was appropriate to the customs and character of the people during his epoch modified with time as moral increases. The "eye for an eye" attitude is disappearing due to Jesus's preaching to not return hate with hate because those who kill by the sword will die by the sword—cause and effect again.

The God Moses heard is the same God clergy, mediums, prophets, and so on claim to hear. The voices are those of angels, the Creator doesn't have to talk to anyone. High-level spirits give us His messages, as happened to me, but no one has to believe me.

Moses prepared the path for Jesus to come and add love to His laws, not to destroy them. But even so, it cost Him crucifixion and demonstrated that religion is a blind field in many ways. Ignorance and violence play a big part in it even today, but it is changing from darkness to light in the name of moral evolution.

If I had written this book years ago, my head would have had a premium on it, but now I am just following the recent flow, especially after 9/11 (a 911 emergency call from heaven for us to change for better). Morality is awakening many politicians and religious leaders to see that without love and charity, suffering will be with us not as bad luck but as the effect of a cause.

Death is watching us whether we are religious or not. The fanatics search for cracks in God's preaching of love; they teach of salvation offered according to each one's belief. Almost everyone wants the easy path to eternity, the wide door Christ mentioned, but the real path leads to a narrow door. All religion is responsible for the mythology that brought about 9/11. Smaller versions of the event occur when families' feud and spouses argue, and atomic bombs still threaten us. Meanwhile, houses of God still preach His Word on our own level. The choice of the wrong prophets gave us the creation of the wrong God.

Jesus

Jesus, the man, and Christ, the Spirit, came at a time when humanity was getting ready for love; His mission was to open heaven's door to all, not to promote Christianity or any religion but the understanding that we are all one family and God is our Father. Jesus awakened us to the necessity of being brothers and sisters in God and loving each other or face suffering.

He did not carry a sword; He taught us in parables that love was more powerful than any sword. He taught us why life is as it is—we are born, suffer, and die, but these are just steps we are to take to evolve morally.

When someone sharpens a sword to protect family or country, others do the same, fearing the menace. When love is preached, no one runs for weapons; behind love is peace. When wars end, everyone embraces each other. They turn their swords into plowshares and rebuild what has been destroyed. But peace lasts only a short time because evil is still alive in the hearts of many of us, religious or not, educated or not.

Jesus left us sentences of consolation that help us differentiate between the material and the spiritual. He did not have women because everyone was married to Him spiritually. He respected and understood this world's spirituality, but He was not chosen to be the highlight of the Father of religions. Even today, the true light from heavens is still far off in the galaxies because our hearts are not yet prepared to face its glory.

The Catholic Church doesn't allow its clergy to marry in an attempt to emulate Jesus, but no human can do that completely. Jesus never said men should avoid women; rather, He blessed the marriage union. The Vatican presented to all religions the blessings of marriage, and other Christian denominations' clergy marry; they realize their preachers are not robots. Pope Francis is right; we won't stop pedophilia until Catholic priests can marry.

Jesus never took anything; He only gave. He brought peace where discord reigned and preached that we should love each other. At His time, the multitude was not prepared for morality; they thought of Him as weak, the human lamb of God, and they waited for the Messiah who was a lion to crush their enemies. Many are still waiting for that Messiah as they hold on to their swords.

Spiritually blind humanity holds onto Abraham's materialism to defend their salvation; they consider him the father of religion, not Christ. This allows atheists to view all religion with negativity.

When men came to stone the adulterous woman, Jesus said that the sinless ones among them could do so. They all left quietly. Jesus had put them on the same level as the adulterous woman; none was sinless. They realized it took two to tango. Jesus considered women to be men's equals, not just pieces of his rib because He couldn't find any more mud. Christ preached that we all had a purpose. Man provided the heavy labor while women bore and raised children.

Christ said He came to fulfill and develop the laws for our advancement in morality and evolution; His doctrine of love was the basis for our duties to our Creator and fellow human beings; He didn't claim anyone or Himself as the leader. He combatted rituals and false interpretations but was unable to make people go through a more radical reform; all He could say was, "Love God above all things and your neighbor as yourself," adding this was all the law we needed. Jesus's record is strong because of the scriptures four of His followers wrote and Saint Thomas's testament, which was found in Egypt after World War II, which confirmed Jesus's whereabouts and His preaching.

The lack of spiritual understanding is so strong that Jesus was not and still is not used as the basis for our morality. His death on the cross is considered simply God's choice; He became a substitute at the altar of sacrifice in the place of an animal. He became the Lamb of God because it was God's will, which took away the gift of free will, humanity's creation, not God's.

The well-organized and financially powerful Roman Catholic Church did a great job of bringing the parables and the Sermon on the Mount to all of us; they contain morality and common sense that can cause us to love, but they draw attention to Christ's bloody death. We end up fearing a bloodthirsty God who demands punishment for our sins. Who will be the next on this cross? A lottery will determine that, and that's no joke.

One day, Peter saw Him crying and asked Him why. Jesus said it was because humanity did not understand His message. Humanity still doesn't understand His message. I wonder if Muhammad created Islam to glorify God's grandeur and love and to cover up the image of a bloody, crucified scapegoat of a mad Creator. Fear dominates those who believe the Roman Catholic teaching that Jesus died a horrible death so we could gain salvation. Is salvation from our sins or from our God?

Jesus gave us all the morality we need for our spiritual advancement but was still used as a sacrificial lamb. His moral teachings, not His crucifixion, form the basis of His message. Images of his bloodied body are inhumane; during World War II, the Japanese crucified prisoners. Pictures of such atrocities weren't made public because they were so repellant. How could the crucified body of Christ represent glory? We are still too far away from being civilized to deserve peace while on Earth.

I saw barbaric images of the crucifixion when I was just six, when my mother took me to church. I screamed, and my mother had to take me home. Such scenes turn reasonable people from, not to, religion, or to religions with less blood and more heaven. My experience in that church haunts me to this day and makes me wonder how people can have faith in a God who allowed His Son to be crucified. Evangelicals don't mention the crucifixion of Christ to save the world; they praise God as the Muslims do. I can walk into their prayer places without seeing scenes from a torture chamber to save my soul. Why should the crucified body of Christ be eternally exposed? How many of us have passed this stage of barbarism? I believe not many.

The Soviet Communists closed the doors of churches for seventy-six years; they should have left open the doors of those churches that represented Christ with His arms out to everyone, like the statue of Jesus on the hill in Rio. That's a Christ with a positive message. Jesus is considered weak because He was not a womanizer, carried no sword, and did not wish harm to anyone; He even pardoned his tortures and executioners. The Koran teaches us, "Forgive people in your life, even those who are not sorry for their actions. Holding on to anger hurts you, not them." I feel Christ was deeper into the Koran than I had imagined. He taught that using force resulted only in retaliation. Today, in the Middle East, people blame each other and no one sleeps in peace; they all have their hands on their swords while they hide behind the words of the prophets.

We don't have Christ as our religious basis because we are still on a barbaric level and look just to the material world rather than heaven. Jesus cried at the beach because He knew it would take millennia for men to understand His messages and meanwhile blood would flow in God's name.

Muhammad

He is the fourth great prophet; he came after Jesus. He knew of Jesus as a prophet, but he leaned on Abraham and Moses just as Judaism and Catholicism do because Jesus's life would not be easy to follow. If he had followed Jesus, that would have been made apparent in his moral life; he would have preached a message of love. Let's stopping blaming Muhammad and Jesus for ours inexcusable wrong interpretations due to lack of knowledge of what is moral or not.

Jesus preached the power of the meek; those who rely on the sword just pour gasoline on the fire. But when someone changes from violence to love, the other party has no fuel to increase the fires of hate.

We will know the author by his book. The Koran is a holy book said to have been inspired by God for the benefit of believers, but everyone can benefit from its teaching on love and peace. Just days after 9/11, the Roman Catholic Church in Washington, DC, hosted a gathering of representatives from almost every nation and religion. Many of them spoke words of comfort and peace. The last one, as far I can remember, were spoken by Muslims as "Ave Maria" was playing in the background.

Muhammad did not write the Koran; according to Islam, the Koran was the result of God speaking to Muhammad through an angel and later written by believers. Muhammad wasn't vain; he didn't say he had heard it directly from God. The same occurred with the Bible; the belief is that God inspired its authors as well. I feel my book is a message from God that I wrote in my last years. I hope that many will read it, but I fear few will and much less understand its spiritual nature.

My vision of the emerald-green lights aboard the cruise ship proved to me that God was merciful and would allow me to write about my long life and thoughts, the good and the bad, as lessons to tell everyone to love each other because the law of cause and effect is unchangeable and as our material lives end, our spiritual lives begin. We are spirits that are evolving; our roads can be easy or hard due to our free will, and we are not created bums but as images of Him.

After 9/11, more people desired to learn about the spiritual world. Books on psychics, especially *The Spirits' Book* by Allan Kardec, founder of the spiritualist doctrine (France, 1865), is being bought now more than ever. The Bible, the Old Testament, and the Koran do not stand alone anymore on home bookshelves; they are kept company by other books that teach us about our existence and a merciful God.

Today, I can talk openly anywhere, and the average person today will listen to me far more than the average person would a few years ago. I sell more of my books on the streets than if I had a bookstore. I felt the need to update our spiritual lives even before my daughter's tragic death.

If Muhammad wrote about the suicide as self-sacrifice to give glory to God, that would be satanic preaching, but we cannot judge and condemn what we do not know. Any Muslim will tell you that suicide and murder are the worst sins against God and that anyone who commits these crimes is not a Muslim. Let's not condemn those who aren't here to defend themselves; let's not rely on hearsay; that is not Christ's way. Bad news runs around the world while good news is still tying the laces on its running shoes. Those who entertain gossip and rumor are standing at the gates of hell.

Those who talk against Muhammad and preach hatred of Islam are performing satanic acts and will pay the price for them. The wolf, as Jesus said, comes as a prophet with an evil tongue. After I read the Koran, I decided that Muhammad could not have created the fanatical, unmerciful promise that heaven would be the reward for terrorists; he left beautiful messages of a grandiose, merciful Allah and the universe as the proof of His existence.

Muhammad wisely and sincerely left vanity for those stuck at altars; he sought those who were seeking spiritual truth, not the glamor of earthly lights. He knelt and screamed, "God! You are great!"

What would be wrong about taking out all the distortions in all the holy books and putting Muhammad's beautiful philosophy of God, Moses's incredible Ten Commandments, and Christ's love and compassion into a book entitled, *The Holy Books—The Essence of the Moral Laws by the Great Prophets for Humanity in the Name of Peace and Love*? Muhammad and the other prophets were mediums God used to teach us about His mercy; they interpreted God's messages. I hear spirits occasionally, but I know they don't come directly from God. I know if they come from good or bad spirits based on the message itself. When I heard my daughter's voice, I knew it was her voice, but if not, I would have imaged it was from her because of its beauty.

I don't blame the prophets, the shepherds; I blame the sheep who blindly follow all kinds of preaching, including that which comes from evil or blind shepherds. Terrorists listen to a new leader who comes from the guts of Earth and preaches an unholy confrontation between the Muslim world and the rest of humanity that could be worse than anything in the past.

As time goes on, we will learn more and more until we no longer need holy books; we will begin to *Embraced in Love, We Reach Heaven*, my book I published in 2001, just few months before the World Trade Center tragedy, but that book stays on shelves collecting dust.

19 Power, Hate, and Materialism Hold Back Our Spiritual Evolution

W hat does it mean to have control? Can we control anything we did not create? Can we control others and sleep in peace? Can we fully know why we exist momentarily in a perishable world and our purpose? Can we give hope to those lost in ignorance, or are we just as ignorant though we think we are wise? How can we teach and convince others that life continues after death?

How can we see beyond a lavish funeral and the words spoken there?

How can we convince others that we should share spiritually? That we will not be taking any material goods with us when we die? That lack of love and charity holds us back in our spiritual evolution? Jesus is still on the cross because we hold on to material things. Religion has become a profit-making enterprise that preaches a cruel God we must follow like lambs.

Some impose their control over others in the name of God; they use His name in vain as the winds blow away the dust of generation upon generation. When we finally decide we are the created, not the Creator, we will progress spiritually and put our material considerations down.

We've seen bumper stickers that reflect a lack of love: "My son is an honor student," "My daughter is the princess of beauty." Would people brag if their sons barely had passing grades or their daughters were eyesores? Religious leaders don't spare even God in this matter; they use His name as a common word and claim to be in touch with Him.

All the prophets "heard and spoke" to God, which put Him on our level of idiocy, but I believe He doesn't mind because His law on evolution is equal to all creation. All those claimers from Abraham up to now had and have their share of pains as alerts that something was and is wrong. The only person you will ever hear having seen Satan is me; I've been through some tough experiences but passed the test. I screamed and tried to punch his nose; he evaporated like a burst balloon.

Jesus had His share of difficulties, but He passed the test as well. Were His tests also a challenge for Him, or could He have refused them? He begged God for mercy on our wrongdoings. Did the others? Just read your holy books. Jesus died on the cross asking God to give us a break. The others died, surrounded by women forced to share their beds, contradicting Christ's moral law to give women a share of men's lives as human beings and mothers. He didn't lean on any sword because He didn't wield one.

The material sword rusts alongside the warrior's skeleton, and his spirit is in the mud with him, but spirits of love and charity float to better places where loved ones wait for superior life. Napoleon Bonaparte (1769–1821) said, "Power is my mistress." He's known as a military genius, but he commanded millions to terrible deaths and millions more to suffering. His opponent, the Duke of Wellington, defeated his army of 360,000 souls with a much smaller force and put an end to this unmerciful conqueror's career but at the cost of an ocean of blood and tears. Both bodies rest in sumptuous cathedrals as reminders of the power of the church to accept the power of evil into what are ironically called houses of God.

No one ever thought to bury Mother Teresa's ashes in the famous Notre Dame Cathedral in Paris but in a little chapel somewhere in India. The Arc de Triomphe built in 1806 was meant to satisfy Napoleon's ego. It glorifies a man who brought so much blood and sufferings to our world. What can we expect from Christianity, which glorifies the bloody image of Christ tortured for salvation of the soul, making God a Creator? If it's all true, I'd rather reside in hell. I know, however, that no fire, ice, or time will destroy my spirit because I am a chip of God. Don't worry; we will all have eternal life.

In 1808 in Spain, during the Peninsular War, three hundred thousand French died in battle because of Napoleon's typical audacious decisions. Napoleon looked at his brothers as inferior, irrational beings and had no regard for anyone's suffering, soldiers or civilians.

I visited many churches in Portugal and Russia that still have the scars of vandalism done by Napoleon's soldiers during their occupation, and I heard of the atrocities done to the population, especially to women. I heard that Napoleon ordered his soldiers to never touch any image of Christ or face the whip; maybe Hitler should be honored by the Vatican because he didn't touch any churches. Pope Pius XII used to receive Gestapo officers for dinner because he felt the church had to survive.

The same church that holds Napoleon's bones is the same one in which he was crowned by people, not by God. To reach Him, we need love, a rare commodity in humanity's heart. The one who died to stop humanity's shedding of blood is still nailed to the cross in the houses of God on Earth but is free in the mansions of His Father. I always go back to Rio to see the statue of Christ there; it takes away the pains I've collected over my life. His image gives us hope that life is more than a period on Earth and that we can and must love one another. It offers comfort to the city's twelve million souls who lack so many material goods but are spiritually rich.

Jesus told us to put our treasures in heaven, where no robbers could take them or rust destroy them. This kind of treasure is our behavior as true Christians, Muslims, Buddhists, or members of any other religion that leads us to spiritual happiness following Jesus's path or any path that ends in love and charity. The wrong path leads to altars of sacrifice, blood, and pain. Such barbarism must end.

Non-Christian religions, especially Buddhism, rarely mention Jesus, but their followers do mention Jesus as a source of comfort during their rough moments. A few saints such as Francis of Assisi and others are acclaimed as saviors, but are they? Is Christ our Savior? Let your conscience tell you God's answer to this crucial question. I know the answer; I have nothing to hide. I have never killed, stole, or cheated anyone, but I have been deceived by some people. I have survived, however, and have pity on those who have deceived me as I saw their lives end in chaos.

20 The Bible of the Third Millennium

All the centuries of wars, revolutions, terrorism, earthquakes, tsunamis, fires, hurricanes, plagues, droughts, famines, and other disasters haven't united religions under one roof. This fact is the mother of all reasons to create one book, *The Reason Book*, the bible of the third millennium. Some have suggested I write it, but should I? I'm reluctant to write it not because my time is running out but because I fear such a book would just gather dust. However, what will turn the uneducated into teachers? And how can our cries be heard by Him? Who knows? Maybe the *THE AGE OF REASON - 2015* will open the door of hope as I believe I will not be around materially, but spiritually in the ever present-time.

Jesus taught that we were not here simply to be born, suffer, and die but to evolve spiritually. In Mark 2:21–22, Jesus taught that it was a waste of time and effort to try to change old sayings: "Do not put new wine in an old barrel because the wine will burst the barrel and the wine and the barrel will be lost." He also taught, "When mending an old clothe, the mend will stay while the cloth will be gone."

This reminds me of the holy books that pounded on the same interpretations but did not take into consideration the giants leaps in science and philosophy we have made. The Koran, written centuries after the New Testament, caused Islam to grow more than any other religion not because it is perfect but because it gives more up-to-date reasons and is not represented by the crucified, bloody body of a man who holds the keys to heaven. Allah is an acclamation of a splendorous, eternal life that does not require a crucifixion.

After my mother led me home from church because I was crying at the sight of the crucified Jesus, she started what we called "our home meeting with God." In a few months, we had more than a hundred people discussing only Jesus's parables and the Sermon on the Mount, as everyone felt peace and love. They developed more faith and respect for our Creator and friendship for all. Back then, in the forties, there were no Muslims around, but if there had been, I know I would have found my way to a mosque where I could chant for a place in the sun.

Carol's husband, Galil, taught us how profound and rational Islam was; Muslims worship God and esteem Muhammad as a man of God. They consider Jesus as the prophet of love; He died on the cross rather than raise a sword and by so doing didn't fail to conquer hell. Words of our Egyptians friends. I wonder when the Vatican will let go of its image of a bloody Jesus and replace it with an image of a Jesus who offers hope of a better day and an afterlife in the universe of a bloodless Creator. That would glorify the church, and I'd be the first to trumpet it.

If I were an alien who stumbled across an image of a Christ who had been killed so His blood would save us, I'd hop back into my spaceship and leave immediately. Mosques, on the other hand, praise the beauty of God's heaven and earth. Worshippers leave mosques with smiles, while worshippers leave churches with fears. In a mosque in Istanbul, I knelt on a rug and bowed to the ground in deference to our Creator, and I was surrounded by people who were doing the same. If I had been required to kneel before the pope when I met him, my twenty-minute interview would have lasted twenty seconds. I would have raced outside and told God, "Thank you for having created me as a chip of yourself."

But nothing is perfect on Earth. I would run just as fast from Mecca if I were required to throw stones at the pillar that represents the devil. That's because coming from a red-skinned family, I might be mistaken for him. Many are killed during this barbaric, nonsensical ritual as the result of the law of cause and effect and a lack of spirituality. A proverb in Spanish says that trying to bring some sense to someone not prepared to understand is like "harvesting in the sea"; we waste our efforts when we face people with blind faith.

The Israelis are still holding on to the *eruv*, the traditional extension of their homes for religious purposes, as they did millennia ago. They are simply doing what they had been instructed to do by their parents, who had learned it from their grandparents, and so on back for millennia. But their spiritual education will have to continue if they want to live with their neighbors, the Palestinians, and share the same water and air with them. They will all have to learn to live as brothers and sisters under the same God.

If combined, science, philosophy, and religion could be our guide to an era free of war and other human maladies. Earth offers all we need, but we must tend to our need for our daily bread. We can all see the emerald-green light I saw on that cruise ship and come to an understanding of our existence.

21 Brutality and Misleading Education

Terrorism today is the same as it was yesterday. The Romans used to "pass the sword" on the population of conquered cities. During World War II, the Japanese army killed almost all the people in Manila before the Americans liberated the city. I think that the atomic bomb was a small evil that prevented a much larger evil, but in seconds, hundreds of thousands were killed by atomic bombs dropped on Nagasaki and Hiroshima—women and children but few combatant men.

Every nation has the right to protect itself, but we have to remember that our attackers are humans, not aliens. How can we beg God for deliverance from the calamities that come our way if we're simultaneously chopping heads off in the name of patriotism and religion? Whole populations suffer because of the madness of their governments.

During the raids on German cities such as Dresden (where 135,000 died and 80 percent of the city was destroyed) and Hamburg (where 50,000 died in firebombing), civilians paid the price for the atrocities committed by their government. When there is no love, no solutions will be found. Today, Japan and Germany are among the first to raise their flags for peace as sufferings came as lessons.

Those committing carnage usually pay the supreme price on the altar of blood as a divine penalty and a moral lesson. Religion as part of humanity's creation has no moral right to intervene in military affairs; it is to remain neutral and help bury the dead. At least religions don't carry weapons anymore; if they don't carry swords, no swords will strike them, but being neutral is not helping being a good Samaritan as the suffering will endure.

Earth is still far away from beaming its occupants to any paradise because

God has taped our negative behavior; that's why He keeps His distance and allows His creation to navigate by its free will until reason takes over. He can wait because the past is yesterday and the present is as eternal as He is, and we have no place to hide from Him. We have made our hell ourselves.

Armies have always demonized their enemies based on their holy books. David was good because he was in God's army and Goliath was bad because he was the enemy. But when the battle is over, all the bodies left behind mingle.

Al-Qaida uses its holy book to recruit terrorists just as Germany and Japan used theirs to further their aims, but the members of al-Qaida will face punishment for their behavior; they will have to answer to the Lord. No matter whose book is followed, differences will always arise because people tend to blindly follow their traditions. Cynically, morals are still so low that religion tries to take that into consideration. If religions were moral enough, they would try hard to change society and not follow its flow. Religion has the creativity to suit its material purposes, but one day, that will change. Humanity will be brought to its knees by calamities that it has brought about. Rivers are drying, lakes are disappearing, and pollution is out of control.

According the world press a group of Christians killed seven hundred Muslims in Lebanon when the PLO moved out, and the killing was blessed by the military power. But up to now, no one, not even the Vatican, said that those assassins were not Christian because Christians wouldn't kill. But Western armies have chaplains to bless the soldiers who kill and die, and the Roman Church was too busy covering up the sexual abuse by its clergy; those in high ranks were having fun with others' children because they didn't have their own.

A clear example of fanaticism is 9/11. Bin Laden, proclaiming to be a Muslim, used the Koran to foment a global war, and here in the West, Protestant pastor Franklin Graham, son of Billy Graham, used the Bible to keep those fanatics on their warpath. What a combination of inflammatory elements! (See *Time* magazine, December 10, 2001, last page.)

22 God's Mini Bible

Love each other and live as a perfect family. Jesus and Muhammad gave you the instructions; follow them and experience miracles. My question is, where is God's love? God is love, and we are here to learn how to love and how to demonstrate it. We must love each other to conform to God's will or there will be no peace on Earth.

How can we control our uncontrollable nature? We are out of control, and we have made our planet a world of incertitude. Our suffering teaches us to seek love; freedom from suffering is a reward, not a handout from our Creator. The only handout we have is our free will; that's our chief gift from God that will allow us to evolve spiritually. We can plead with God all we want, but He won't interfere due to our free will until we purify ourselves. That's when the gates of heaven will open wide and it begins here.

The truth is that God hears us all but doesn't always answer the way we want Him to. Faith healers, however, will have you believe they can work miracle cures. You see the healed jumping up and down on TV, but the government won't put its nose into religion; our elected officials want votes, even if they come from those with simple blind faith. Meanwhile, those who weren't healed will still be invited to revivals and healings so they can donate more money; the religion machine will make sure its wheels are well greased. God can perform miracles, but He can't be forced to perform miracles; He'll perform the miracles He wants to perform.

We can lose a leg or a hand and survive, but if we lose our head in a guillotine, our spirits will leave our bodies. Let's say science discovers a way to keep just a head alive; would that head still be a human? Our bodies are wonderful instruments for us as spirits, a spectrum of an eternal light but formed as our bodies so we can differentiate between Joe and Mary.

We are awake when we put aside our old, defunct, barbarian beliefs and embrace today's science and philosophy and Jesus's basic ideas of a fair society based in love and charity. Muhammad is also a good example of someone glorifying our Creator. Their example can keep us from battling over pieces of land and fighting over whose religion is the right one.

Today's religions are as blind as is humanity because human beings created them. God created us and gave us the path to spiritual evolution with unchangeable laws of justice. Then He gave us free will, but most of us don't give that a thought because deep thinking is not on our agenda.

God doesn't interfere with our gladiatorial urges; He knows we will eventually educate ourselves. We keep Jesus's body on the cross, run to Mecca, and hold the Torah as sacred; God will just keep recording our activity and will judge us accordingly. We can kill ourselves as many times as it takes for us to learn because death is just the liberation of the soul back to the spiritual stage and then back to the soul stage with another body with a greater or a lesser number of moral debts. The Roman Catholic Church rejected the concept of reincarnation and made it a matter of one life and then heaven or hell. The idea of flesh burning in hell for eternity opened the way to burning heretics at the stake. The church called it the fire of redemption, as if saying, "Join us or face the flames."

Later, the church found out that the fear of burning in hell was too dramatic, so it came up with the idea of purgatory, a hell lite, so to speak. Great marketing, but Muslims are now gaining a greater share of the market.

Buddhism believes in reincarnation, and many Westerners agree, but those who practice Buddhism keep their mouths shut. It began in the West with *The Spirits' Book* by Allan Kardec in the nineteenth century and is spreading like the wind in Brazil and other Latin American countries. Brazil's 220 million souls are not filling Catholic churches because Spiritism offers a new afterlife that doesn't include heaven or hell. Islam is also going strong in Brazil as Arabic immigration is increasing now as Arabs run from conflicts. Jews are also leaving Israel for safer grounds in the United States and South America, especially Brazil.

The promoters of hell are losing business; they should come up with a cool-hell theory with visitations allowed. That sounds like a joke, but huge religion institutions need the income for a great material life.

Realities put bread and butter on the table while theories are make-believe. Please don't tell me yours dreams and I won't tell you mine. Don't wait for your dreams to come true because death will come first. I heard whispered by the wind as I faced Hurricane Katrina in August 2005 in south Florida, "Faith and hope stroll holding hands as good friends, not to lean on each other to keep their balance."

Death means nothing to God, but it means much to human beings so steeped in the material world. The flesh is perishable; we don't know which moment will be our last. Our bodies are holy temples but not our eternal homes, which are the infinite, colorful galaxies dominating the eternal, illuminated dark matter with no beginning or end. Alleluia! (I like to say that when the pastor says anything or even sneezes as he looks at me confirming it)

23 Jesus Didn't Change the Law but Added Love to It

"I didn't come to change the law, but to add love to it," said Jesus. He didn't want to open a new church or be nailed to the cross to save us from our devilish behavior and make the Creator a satanic vampire we would fear. He didn't want us to kneel to the Roman Catholic Church for salvation because that would contradict all His preaching. He came here to add love to any religion's beliefs or individuals, but He didn't have to change any religious laws; love would make them unnecessary.

They crucified Him for his moral preaching that didn't fit their moral evolution; He was hurting the religion "business" by contradicting a fearful God and the wrong use of tithes to build gorgeous churches and having a boundless society life .

How could Christ order up a new religion worshipping a merciful God who allowed His Son to be crucified? My wife and I have visited mosques with no altars, no images of pained saints, and we felt peace. We prayed, "Thank you, almighty Father."

If Christ came to change the law instead of adding love to it, He would have been a false prophet like many who have made the world suffer. Jesus didn't make a mistake; it was humanity that didn't understand His message because of its lack of spiritual evolution. The Sermon on the Mount as the basis for God's kingdom on earth is not adopted by religious leaders because its beatitudes don't fit the lifestyles of those they preach to. They represent the crucified Jesus, the glorification of the body for the material world and not the spirit in heaven.

Jesus came here to teach us, not to offer His body as salvation because that was impossible; He came to advise us on how we could deserve a place in the sun, or better yet, a room in His Father's mansion—no blood involved.

24 The Solution to Water Scarcity

The religious leaders who mention a fiery hell (which wouldn't burn spirits anyway) because we didn't behave or worse didn't belong to a specific congregation or didn't tithe make Earth a living hell for us.

God is flooding our cities; is this a punishment from Him or a challenge from Him? I found the solution, so keep reading for it. I spent hours reading about how God is pouring rain on cities such as São Paulo while the rivers are down 30 to 60 percent and unable to move turbines to create electricity, which is causing blackouts in the country. The Brazilian government distributes sewer water minimally treated to the residents of the favelas, the slums, and people there are suffering and dying from diarrhea and infections. They take showers in rain, which also washes out the spaces on streets they use as toilets. The government tries to look good by distributing packets of purification powder. The meat industry is suffering due to the lack of water for the cattle, which foul what water there is. The Amazon forest, the lungs of the earth, is being destroyed for its timber and for grazing land for cheap beef. This is an international crime against humanity, but I will not be here to see the perpetrators of that crime prosecuted if any will be jailed.

God is not putting the water on the right place—so say the Australians, Brazilians, Koreans—all earthlings. Australia's lack of rain for the last four years has prompted it to build the biggest water desalination plant that will produce very expensive water and pollution as well. People in areas of the world with no underground water pray for rain for their daily bread, but prayers alone doesn't work it must be together with good deeds.

We need to perform good deeds to reach the favor of our Creator, but without love and charity, prayer means nothing; it is just words whispered into the wind. I asked our Creator why He was flooding cities rather than reservoirs and fields, but He didn't respond because He knows I know the answer. Satan gets the blame for all this from the pulpit, but we have to be more faith-filled, read the Bibles, and bring more people to God.

Though the clouds are water hanging over our heads, we cannot control them. And why does the ocean have to be so salty? Only God knows. He didn't pollute our water sources; we did that with our bad planning and greed. Our Creator gave us the intelligence we need to stop polluting our air and to start using our water much more efficiently, for instance, by diverting rainfall not into sewers but into reservoirs for crop irrigation. We are not behaving like Bedouins, who can live on not much water daily; we die if we can't take half-hour showers.

God is washing the cities and roads, but He wants us to use our brains to use His rain wisely. He has given us all we need, but we must learn to use it wisely and humbly and with love.

25 Blind Faith Is Our Worst Enemy

You have blind faith when you have a belief that you never question. You're like a mule following a carrot dangling just in front of him until he stumbles and breaks a leg.

To pray is to try to reach the spiritual world by words, but "trying to" contact and "not reaching" are the same thing; our souls are spiritually almost powerless due to our lack of understanding and morality.

Don't believe that praying is just a matter of saying words. Words aren't deeds; they are irrelevant sounds if they aren't judged worthy by our Creator. Many of us mistakenly believe prayer should be directed only to God, but the Creator also listens to His messengers such as Jesus, the saints, and the prophets. It's beyond our capacity to fully grasp the complexity of creation even with our common sense and reason. Faith is the greatest energy that will connect us to the cosmos, but it's not the principal instrument that will make it possible—prayer backed up by charity and love is. God wants more than words; He allows us to suffer what we suffer so we can grow spiritually. We will receive what we morally deserve just as we can give only what we have. If we don't pity others, why would our Creator pity us?

I heard a TV preacher praying to God in front of a large audience. He wanted God's forgiveness for not being able to take the gospel to all the people of the world because he succumbed to Satan. He said that the millions of dollars he was receiving were not enough; he needed more money from them to spread the Word. The audience immediately opened their wallets and offered money for God's victory and Satan's downfall. I felt sorry for God and pity for Satan, who gets blamed for almost everything.

The majority of us believe what we believe and think others couldn't possibly be in possession of the truth. We'd do well to study what other religions say and quit thinking and acting in blind faith; we have to love others rather than condemn them or their religion or politics.

Blind faith is the worst enemy of evolution; it keeps us in ignorance about what's happening outside our little worlds. I've spoken to thousands of people in many countries, and some have told me that life in their countries was wonderful, more than they could have ever hoped for, and that they didn't see the need to travel to neighboring countries. They were happy with their inherited beliefs and attitudes, and they planned to pass them on to their sons and daughters. But those sons and daughters will not see a broader reality due to such a narrow and loveless attitude. What we preach is wrong if we stay put in our beliefs and never upgrade them in light of other beliefs. We will simply drift until we crash on the rocks of suffering.

Religion says that to have faith is to believe, to follow without doubt. Catholics and Protestants mistakenly call themselves true Christians, but true Christians follow Jesus's teaching, which precedes Catholicism and Protestantism.

Education is the key to moral evolution, and religion is instruction or teaching doctrine to people, but to teach doctrine without an open mind is not to educate; it makes people see no farther than the tips of their noses.

To be educated is to go inside the conscience to find God. Those who preach that God is to be feared don't help those with no love in their hearts. People kill others in the name of religion, but their preaching is nothing but words lost in the wind. My book reflects our free will flying free of a cage. Thomas Paine stated we can enslave others' bodies but not their souls.

Blind faith is simply ignorance that gives me the chills because it's not based on wisdom, which we have and should learn to increase. God wants us to love and be charitable. We have the wisdom to treat each other with kindness and live as a peaceful family, but that's still a far-off dream. Our need for armies, police, and hospitals is evidence that we're not doing our homework.

One good example are the blind faith of today terrorists that do atrocities with open heart as heavens approves it, but is easy to go to from soul to spirit and the spiritual world law is correct and doesn't lean on blind faith, but justice to all related in good deed. To have blind faith is absolute ignorance with his mind blocked away from knowledge and inactive to seek better consciousness.

26 My Answer to Atheists

What is an atheist? For several nights, I read hundreds of atheists' quotes on the Internet and concluded that they were intelligent people who had read about, spoken to, and listened to believers in God and had concluded that believers had based their beliefs on a book that boasts of a cruel, bloody Creator we'd be better off without and the brutality of humanity.

The Internet is like a giant confessional; I consider it a great leap in the direction of moral evolution as I sense I am not alone in my thinking. We are evolving in our attitudes toward women and people of different races, and evil is losing ground. The Internet can promote common sense, reason, and critical thinking, which will make us all less susceptible to manipulation. Promoting the concept of a God we should fear makes a mockery of faith. I'll pound on this point until another William Moreira show up to rescue us from suffering.

But God does exist; His universe is evidence of this even though not all of us have the IQ to comprehend that fact. Some learn to read at age three while others spend their lives trying to add two and two. But don't worry; after we leave our bodies, we will live as spirits for eternity and will know that two plus two equals four and much more in heaven.

27 Everything Is a Mystery to the Created

"To be or not to be" is the question; "to be born or not to be born" is the mystery. This was whispered to me when I was aboard a cruise ship. Atheists don't think they have a future after death, but in all my years of flying, I never met a pilot who was an atheist. If one would have been found among us, we'd clip his or hers wings on the spot and take a car because we knew God wouldn't be in the copilot's seat.

The first quote is our choice, but the second is a gift to us. There is no choice because the decisions have already been made, and not only for our existence. The path to follow is on Earth; we have free will but we also have rules and regulations.

As I have aged, I see more clearly the horizon of an afterlife. I know I'll be landing pretty soon. A crowd will be waiting for me with good news and directions down a new path on a new stage. I don't know what it will be, but it will be better than life on Earth, where the only guarantee is that we will be born, suffer, and die. However, our intelligence and common sense tell us there's a future beyond death as well as a Creator.

I know of a grandmother who went to Miami to live with her grand-daughter. The grandmother brought her dog that in just a short time, due to nature's calls, ruined the granddaughter's rugs. The granddaughter replaced that dog with a small dog. I felt sorry for the grandmother, but the grand-mother began to love the small, trained dog. We'll all ultimately spiritually evolve and leave behind our irrational ideas.

Free will is the greatest gift we have; it distinguishes us from the rest of creation. Only the dull witted can look at a great painting and think it just dropped from the sky. We might not believe in God because we've never seen His face, but He doesn't mind because He's perfect and knows we will ultimately come to know the grandeur of His universe.

Our life on Earth is a balloon that can burst at any time; I've seen enough deadly accidents to convince me of this. I witnessed a horrible accident in Switzerland. A driver who was too busy talking to his girlfriend hit a seventy-year-old man even though I had screamed for him to look out. My wife and I were actually splashed with the victim's blood. That was fifty-three years ago, but I can never forget that horrible scene. I want my readers to take seriously what I write about the necessity of evolving spiritually before their time comes to move on to the spiritual world.

I've learned that when our bodies have been mangled in an accident, our spirits stick around for a while until an "angel" comes to explain our transition from the material to the spiritual world. Someone who had witnessed my daughter's death told me she had been killed instantly by the truck that ran her over. I was comforted somewhat to have learned this. When our time is up, we have no way to extend it. Death is ultimately a part of life, and it can occur in a split second.

I received a visit at home from someone from Belleview Hospital in New York the day after Carol died. He kindly expressed his sorrow and explained he conducted research on deaths such as Carol's. He told me that he studied the brains of accident victims and people who had died of, say, natural causes. He told me that he had noted differences between the brain cells of those who were suddenly confronted with death and those who knew it was coming.

He told me that those who faced sudden death but survived were affected for years as being dead; it was as if they were alive but dead and could fade away in just a matter of months because their brains were no longer able to sustain life.

Two months later, the same gentleman asked me to meet him at a death phenomenon research center, where I learned a lot about death and our spiritual nature. I never expected such a kind reception at a research center or what happened next. He gave me an envelope, which I took home to read. Inside was a check for $1,000 and a note that read, "This thousand dollars is for you, your wife, and your grandson. Please have a great Manhattan dinner in the name of your beautiful, charismatic daughter Carol. She will be in our hearts eternally as an angel."

A few years later, a friend told me that his mother had been hit by a car while crossing the street in Newark and was in a coma. I visited her in the hospital, and the scene reminded me of my experience with Carol's death. She was emotionless; her body was there but not her soul. She was being fed intravenously; she died a few weeks later. It brought to mind the other accidents I had witnessed and reminded me of the universal law of cause and effect.

28 February 5, 1996: The Ghost of Consolation

"Pappy, I finally brought the most important video cassette in our life. A movie that hits our hearts, *Ghost*. It affirms that death is just exchanging the carnal body for the spiritual body."

Carol told me this cheerfully, not knowing her days on Earth were numbered, but mercy was available in the form of even a movie that offered hope. "Let's watch it tonight," she said.

"Carol, my angel, how many times have you seen it?"

"At least four, but I need you to watch it because it could come in handy one day. Death can take anyone by surprise, and this movie can help souls as spirits."

After dinner, she dragged me and Christopher, her eight-year-old son, to the TV. We ate a creamy strawberry cheesecake she had made based on a recipe I had, but hers was better than mine. It became known as "Carol's angel cheesecake," and so many had asked her for the recipe that she had had it printed up.

Ghost hit people's hearts, particularly those who had been wounded by the deaths of loved ones. The movie offered hope and consolation to adults and children alike. Carol was affirming the fact that God allows spirits to help people realize they have to take the invisible world seriously. I feel she was giving me a warning as her time with us was approaching its end.

"Daddy, I think the movie gives consolation to everyone when death strikes. We all become lost in our grief, even knowing we will all go thought it, but it is good to know that we can educate ourselves about it. It's insurance for the bad moments such as sicknesses. Accidents can happen any time, but we have to live before we can die."

I had one eye on the screen and the other on Carol; I felt something was going to happen. She smiled many times, but her face was full of concern. She was getting closer to me while she had her son on her lap.

When the movie ended, she looked at me as if trying to tell me something important. I could feel something wrong was going to happen. I asked her, "My dear baby, please tell me, are you sensing your time with us is getting shorter? Do you have a serious medical problem? If you do, I promise to keep the secret as long as you want."

She held my hand for an eternal minute. Her face was down. I could see a drop of a pearl rolling down her face. She said, "Pappy, sometimes we feel like we had a bad dream, as if death will take us away. This presentiment has been haunting me for months, and even now, I drive under the speed limit, always on the right, and pay attention to any details that could be lethal.

"I'm worried that I'm getting paranoid. As I go to work in Times Square, I go for a few minutes daily to a beautiful, historic Catholic Church and even to Galil's mosque once a month to say to God that if possible, I want to see my grandson grow up. Now, I'm thinking about what *Ghost* is teaching us, that no one vanishes with death. When there is love involved, we'll meet again because spirits can be in touch with souls."

One week later, on the ice-cold morning of February 5, 1996, she crossed on the green pedestrian light and was hit by a huge newspaper truck that had run the light. The driver alleged that his brakes had frozen, but that was proven false. He finally admitted to running the light.

When we have to go, nothing will stop it. Her death was a confirmation of karma, destiny, and mission, a trio as real as can be for those who seek spirituality rather than black holes for moral comfort.

She died instantly as a young beautiful lady, not a pile of wrinkles alone and waiting to be released by death from a godless world in which hope doesn't exist.

The thousands who attended her funeral saw a pink blanket on top of her casket. On top of that was a three-by-three-foot portrait of her I had painted when she was twenty and another I had done when she was six for her birthday. I made copies of it and sent them to all who had signed the condolence book, even though that took me three months. I told them all that Carol was officially our angel and that she was still here to give us all hope.

For almost four months, people from everywhere rang our bell and gave us roses or lilies and embraced us. They said that angels came back to comfort us when a tragedy is involved, and she was one of them.

At the main office at Marriot Marquis Hotel in the heart of Manhattan, my wife, Christopher, my daughter's beautiful, eight-year-old, charismatic son, and I met for coffee and cake. Thousands of her colleagues wanted to meet her son and the parents of an employee who had become the angel of the eighth floor. Her smile, manners, and appearance had won them over.

The general manager said that without Carol, it was as if the lights had gone off. He said it taken months for the staff and many guests to get back to normal lives, as she was always mentioned.

Twenty-one years later, I had lunch at the Marriot Marquis's famous Encore, where Carol had been the star. I asked the new crew about her and showed her photos, but they all said, "Carol who?" The present is all we have. The past is history, and the future is unknown. Nonetheless, as Lavoisier taught us, nothing is lost—it's only transformed.

My wife watched *Ghost* for many years as a consolation message from Carol. Whenever anyone was hurting, she'd have him or her over for tea and a slice of Carol's strawberry cheesecake that I'd bake. My wife would play the movie, and it consoled many people many times.

She told me she thought that Stephen Hawking was being punished for spreading his hopeless message that lacked love. "Pappy," she'd tell me, "we must have compassion for the ignorant ones. They suffer because they don't believe in the Creator. I feel sorry for his condition, but it isn't God's fault. He played with fire and got burned."

Those with faith believe heaven is waiting for them. They have hope even though at times it seems to be just a cork they've grabbed onto while drowning. It's better than nothing, and at best, it's a consolation. Religion is a necessity for those seeking answers to what lies beyond death; they receive no help from science's telescopes and microscopes because such man-made instruments cannot answer their questions. I have a feeling that aliens could visit us after we stop killing each other to help us. I hope they aren't scared off by our low levels of spirituality and morality.

I worry for our descendants; the water we leave them is diminished and misused, and the air is polluted by smokestacks. It takes lobsters seven years to reach two pounds, and it takes trees so much longer to bear fruit. Our earth is fragile. The geniuses among us, of course, can simply jump into the spaceship Enterprise when things get too tough, but what about the rest of humanity?

29 I Rest My Pen

It is marvelous to "walk" on the water of our imagination. I get that feeling when I fly; I use metal wings to float on the air and feel like an angel. I'm on my own, free from all of life's nightmares and somewhere between heaven and hell.

Many friends, parents, wife, sons, grandsons, and thousands of others tried to persuade me all those years that I was playing with fire trying to reach God and wasting my time on a lost cause—my writing—because few people would read it. Not even Jesus had been successful at teaching others.

I smiled. I said I read and wrote only in the wee hours, which allowed me to earn my daily bread during the rest of my time. Besides, I wanted more than my daily bread; I wanted food for my soul. I sincerely believed it would bring understanding and relief to a world about why life is the way it is. We didn't just jump into existence by a freak accident of nature or a huge explosion; we were the plan of a supreme intelligence that always existed, the Creator of the big bang. We are His family; we can think and wonder about Him. Everything is so marvelous that we can only accept it. We can entertain theories to keep us happy and entertain us as long as those theories aren't harmful. Some people say that to dream is to live, but I think that to live is to dream.

We all came from an ovum, even Adam and Eve. It takes us nine months to become flesh and bone; our bodies are homes for our souls for a short time during which we are to learn to love and to evolve morally. We then depart on our eternal journeys, and my time for that is coming up. Let's all be happy that we're not just piles of atoms that cannot imagine our Creator.

I did all I could to express what's in my mind about how we shouldn't offend others and how we should try to discover why we are and why life is the way it is, how we should learn to love and direct ourselves and others to a better world.

I give hope, which is what everyone is after. I have repeatedly picked up my Parker 51 pen beginning when I was a twenty-one-year-old professional journalist. Since then, I didn't give my pen a day off. God doesn't stop, so why should I? You can take that as a joke if you want; we can't be serious all the time, even at funerals.

Our material life depends on the little bit of freshwater we have left as our planet travels at 108,000 kilometers per hour tilted at a 23-degree angle and spinning around daily as it travels through dark matter. We don't lose our balance because someone is minding the whole process with perfect engineering, greasing its gears, and keeping it all on track even while we sharpen our swords and kill each other in the name of our Creator.

This will sound like a joke, but I'm the only one in the universe who feels sorry for God; our behavior is worse than that of Roman gladiators or hyenas on the prairies of Africa, and it has turned His hair white. When I hear, "This is my blood; drink it for your salvation," I get sick. I've seen enough blood shed in my life. I drove an ambulance in New York when I was twenty-four and saw way too much blood shed by people who had been in accidents or gun battles, and I've seen my own blood, particularly right after I cut off four of my fingers at a butcher's shop. I can't think of shed blood as a way to salvation.

I remember seeing on Brazilian TV a beautiful young woman who was in a wheelchair singing and tossing kisses to an audience that was applauding this angel (her body is of a four years old child). She spoke about how great it was to be alive. She said we're all eternal spirits in a marvelous universe. I felt ashamed to have had any doubts about God's mercifulness. Our journey to spiritual evolution is a long but necessary road to the infinite, but walking hand in hand with others and with God will make it that much easier.

I was asked once: Is there a hidden place from God? And I said no, because every corner are rounds, just like atoms!

As for the title of this book is a victory for all of us, because I just wrote the manuscript without a heading for the first time, and I did it in less than 60 hours in the cruiser ship Lirica. As the editors referred it as THE AGE OF

REASON I called them saying it was a mistake as THOMAS PAINE wrote with this title in three parts in 1794, 1795 and 1807. They argued that is no copywrite for titles and my manuscript is unique as unique is writing of Paine. I hope sooner than later I will encounter Paine and then I had fulfill my dreams, and why not because to dream goodness with open eyes is just like hope.

I mention God 271 times, Jesus name 107 times and reincarnation only twice, please don't ask me if I believe in the spiritual dimension or if there is an afterlife because I will tell those to read this book again or any of my previous books.

I never say good-bye because good-bye is forever. I say so long; that means we'll meet again somewhere because we are always united in the present time. Email me if you'd like to discuss this more, particularly what I've written about the concept of time. I want you to find spiritual peace here and in eternity. Time I don't have but I find it to answer those with a sincere thoughts.

—William Moreira

williamcanno@gmail.com

www.williammoreiraauthor.com

30 The Message of the Millennium

Lord, my God! I have walked lands, navigated seas, flown over horizons, conquered forests, climbed mountains, and worked hard for my daily bread. I have studied, researched, learned, taught, and suffered to feel the meaning of "love one another" and to learn why life is as it is.

Now, my Lord, my eyes are tired, my legs are too weak to take long walks, my skin is dry and wrinkled, and my vocal cords are unable to voice warnings to your children.

Above my white head appears a smiling lad. He's happy, almost angelic, and is floating clearly in front of me as part of my thoughts. I'm content as I confront radiant, positive spirituality. I ask our Lord, "Who is this fascinating lad?"

The Lord answers, "This lad is you reflected in the mirror of truth. He shows what you offered in the name of love and charity. This fluid image of energy is your eternal spirit that never tires, ages, or dies. What you gave as seedling, you are harvesting now, and now you belong to the celestial world, where heaven has no limits."

31 Moses's Ten Commandments and My Eleventh Commandment

Jesus's parables and the Sermon on the Mount are spiritual guidance for everyone, as are the moral laws of progress and Moses's Ten Commandments written millennia ago. I have spiritually received an amendment necessary as we change our behavior in society.

1. "Thou shalt have no other gods before me." (More than one God would be no God at all.)
2. "Thou shalt not make unto thee any graven image." (God has no portrait to be adored because He is in our conscience.)
3. "Thou shalt not take the name of the Lord in vain." (Do not swear lies; tell the truth in His name.)
4. "Remember the Sabbath day, to keep it holy." (Everyone deserves at least one day off after working six days, even slaves in the past.)
5. "Honor thy father and mother." (When parents get older and have no more physical protection or cannot support themselves, many sons and daughters abuse them because of the lack of love.)
6. "Thou shalt not kill." (If this were in everyone's heart, there would be no wars or assassinations, and Rome's Colosseum would have being a sport arena; the only killing allowed would be in self-defense when our lives are in peril.)
7. "Thou shalt not commit adultery." (This is wrongly interpreted as being only for men; it's also for women.)
8. "Thou shalt not steal."

9. "Thou shalt not bear false witness against thy neighbor." (Lying can destroy someone's life.)

10. "Thou shalt not covet." (This is to crave or desire something another has; it could be jealousy of someone's success.)

11. "Thou shalt not desire another's man's woman or another woman's man." (Today's equal-rights laws give women rights in male-dominated society, and some women use that freedom to cover immoral sexual behavior. That destroys the blessed concept of family and brings anarchy to the moral laws affecting spouses, children, parents, and friends that might not be repaired for generations.)

Send any comments to williamcanno@gmail.com. I'll do my best to answer.

32   A Personal Prayer to God

God, our celestial Father, You are kind, and You are heaven almighty who gives strength to those going through difficult times and gives light to those who seek truth. Give us all compassion and charity.

God! Give to the traveler a guiding star; to the afflicted, consolation; to the ill, peace.

God! Give to the guilty regret; to the spirit, the truth; to the child, guidance; to the orphan, a family.

Lord! May Your mercy extend itself over everything You have created.

Give mercy, O Lord, to those who do not know You and hope and understanding to those who suffer.

May Your kindness permit compassionate spirits to spread peace, hope, and faith over everyone.

God! One stroke of lightning, one spark of Your love, can inflame the earth. If You let us drink from the fountain of Your abundance, Your infinite kindness, all tears will be dried and all pain will be alleviated.

Only one heart, only one thought, will elevate us to You—the recognition of love. Like Moses on the mountain, we wait for You with open arms.

O Power! O Kindness! O Beauty! O Perfection! We want in some way to reach Your mercy for our wrongs.

God! Give us heartfelt charity, give us faith and understanding, and give us the simplicity that will make our souls the mirror in which You are reflected.

This prayer is the beginning of our contact with the spiritual world and absolute love. Our Creator's love is waiting for us. "My conscience tells me that Paine broke the ice for Kardec's navigation upstream into the difficult water of moral evolution."[1]

The Bible and other holy books preach that faith is the acceptance of the word as true without questioning it. Thomas Paine says reason must come before faith. Nineteenth-century French spiritualist Allan Kardec wrote that faith alone is blind faith if there is no reason.

[1] —from *What Christ, Thomas Paine, and Allan Kardec Want You to Know and Religion Doesn't.*

33

My Easy Potato Pancakes and Apple Sauce Everyone Will Love

- Peel a large potato.
- Skin an onion half the size of the potato.
- Grate potato and onion, and put them in a dry kitchen towel. Wring out as much moisture as you can.
- Put the onion and a potato in a bowl with 2 eggs, 1 tablespoon of flour, and pepper, salt, parsley, cheese, or any other spices and seasonings you like.
- Mix it all with fork or fingers.
- Spoon the mixture into pancake shapes, and sauté (that sounds better than "fry") in oil that is hot but not too hot. Don't use olive oil, as that will leave an oily taste.
- Flip them over after they brown on one side, and let them brown on the other side.

Enjoy with bacon, sour cream, cream cheese, and applesauce (recipe follows).

Apple Sauce
- Peel and chop 8 to 10 small apples.
- Put them in a 1-quart pot with 1 tablespoon of water and 1 table-spoon of sugar.
- Cover and cook over medium heat for about 20 minutes or until tender.

- Whisk with a handheld electrical mixer or mash with a potato masher.

It lasts about a week in the refrigerator, and there are no calories involved because I said so.

I was eight when I learned this recipe from my mother. I honor this recipe among the many I carry around in my mind as a gift from our Creator. We deserve it for all our good deeds.

OIL PAINTINGS

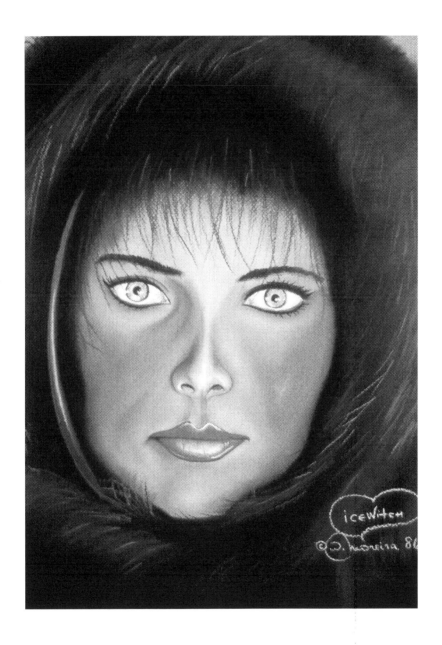

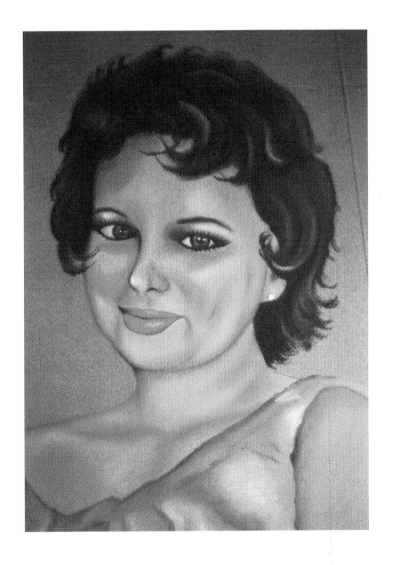

Printed in the United States
By Bookmasters